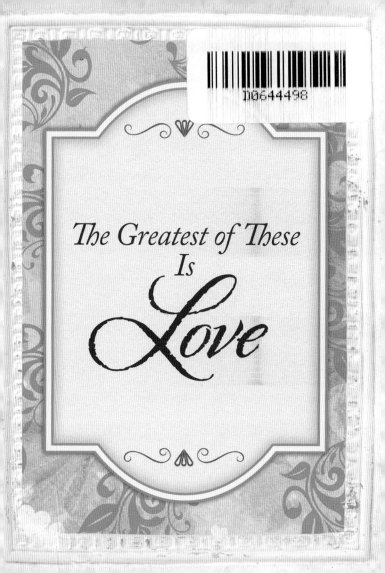

The Greatest of These
Is

Love

Published by Barbour Publishing, Inc., P.O. Box 719, Uhrichsville, Ohio 44683, www.barbourbooks.com

Our mission is to publish and distribute inspirational products offering exceptional value and biblical encouragement to the masses.

Member of the
Evangelical Christian
Publishers Association

Printed in China.

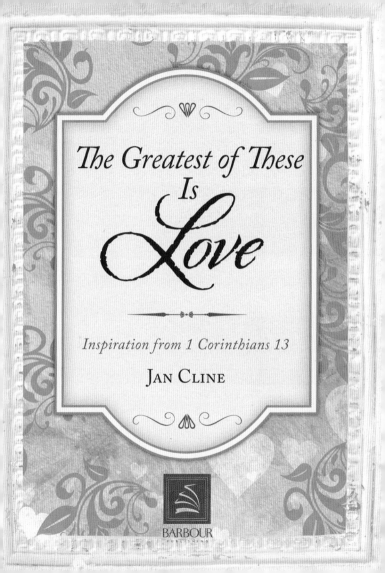

The Greatest of These Is Love

Inspiration from 1 Corinthians 13

JAN CLINE

BARBOUR
PUBLISHING

Contents

Introduction

Of all the chapters in the Holy Bible, 1
Corinthians 13 is perhaps the most beloved.
It has been quoted and referenced for centuries
by Christians all over the world. Yet, how many
of us can say we have eagerly embraced its
standard? Through its poetic verses, God shows
us a paradigm of transforming proportions.

The Greatest of These Is Love charts the
course of our journey to attain charity. The
components of these verses announce the
glory of the great commandments—to love
God and love our neighbor as ourselves.

Where is that constraining,
controlling love that reins in our emotions,
desires, passions, dreams, and ambitions,
holding them tight in a determination that we
will not—no matter what—discredit the ministry
of reconciliation to which God has called us?

KAY ARTHUR, *LORD, GIVE ME A HEART FOR YOU*

More Than Words

A Song of Love

—◆·◆·◆—

If I speak in the tongues of men or of angels,
but do not have love, I am only a
resounding gong or a clanging cymbal.

1 CORINTHIANS 13:1 NIV

If you were a song, what would you sound like? Would you be a solid beat with lots of electric guitar? Perhaps you would send out soft harp music, soothing and serene. How about a tune you can march to or a classical melody of piano and strings? You might be a happy song or a drudging throng of discords.

The world will know you by the song you play. They will listen and wonder how you came to play such a song. Not everyone will like your style, but they will know if it's sincere. They will know if you like music or hate it, and they will wonder why you sound the way you do.

What's behind your song?

If we don't have the love of Christ, our song will only be sound. But when His love permeates the notes and nuance, it will touch the hearts of those who hear it. It's not the song that matters so much, but the love that birthed it. Just as the truest form of melody stirs the emotions of those who hear, so the purest reflection of Christ's love in our lives impacts our observers.

It's not always convenient to take on the form of a harp when we feel like a drum. When we consider the greatest musician of all and the new song He has given us, we will never go back to the discord of loveless words.

The song from our lips will cease. But the love behind the song will last long after the music has faded. The choice to share songs of love is a privilege that requires true diligence. As we deliberately pursue the call to impact our world, we will find our audience.

Truth in All Things

———— ◆◆ ————

Now that you've cleaned up your lives by
following the truth, love one another
as if your lives depended on it.

1 PETER 1:22 MSG

When you think of the word integrity, what comes to mind? It could be that we don't know what it means to truly live with integrity. As Christians, we may believe we automatically walk in integrity because we have the Spirit of God living in us. It feels right to assume our specialness in Christ gives us that upright quality, defining our strength of character. But is integrity proved only by our declaration to be followers of Christ?

Christianity is not the key that unlocks the door of integrity. The definition is not as important as the application. The words we speak express our depth of understanding of this virtue, but in no way guarantee righteousness in the sight of those who are watching us. It's important for us to line up our words with the ongoing flow of actions that give the words life.

A spouse can say "I love you" all day long, but if there is never any outward manifestation of that love, it has no meaning. Service, sacrifice, and practical help make the words believable. It's the same with the world and how they perceive those who spout words of love but never back them up with tangible acts.

A pronouncement of love calls for proof, especially by those who are already skeptical about our intentions, or God's intentions. Our union with integrity can accomplish anything when it's sincerely mixed with words and actions. Integrity? It's not automatic, but it's necessary when it comes to love.

Take Time for Love

---

*Be wise in the way you act toward outsiders;
make the most of every opportunity.*
COLOSSIANS 4:5 NIV

With all the modern conveniences we use in our day,
there are still never enough hours to reach the end of
our to-do lists. It seems as if the technical advances in
the past few decades have not advanced us at all. When
it comes to the really important things in life like love,
peace, rest, and worship, our time for them has been
eaten up. We are so enveloped in learning how to make
life easier, we have no time to enjoy the easy part.

All the virtues Christ admonished us to weave into our being can drown in the sea of today's distractions. The voice of Jesus calling is not heard over the noise of technological toys and necessities. All these things were supposed to provide those extra minutes in the day. But instead of having more time to minister love and grace, we have less.

How does this affect what others see and hear of us? We hope that we will reflect Jesus, but often we only reflect the busyness and mindlessness of a lifestyle that has no time for stillness. We have no time for rest, no time for our brothers and sisters in the faith, and no time for God, so how can we be believable as Christians?

Jesus longs for us to seek refuge from our slavery to high-tech living. When we turn to Him, He will lead us beside the still waters that restore our very souls. We are rescued from the calamity of emotional collapse. Then we are able to be a legitimate extension of our declaration to be Christ followers.

Listen for His Call

I listen carefully to what God the LORD is saying,
for he speaks peace to his faithful people.
PSALM 85:8 NLT

There are many things that block our hearing. Some medications can cause your ears to ring. A cold can plug your ears with congestion, or you may work in a noisy environment. Straining to hear is not just a nuisance, it can be dangerous in some situations.

We don't realize how much we depend on hearing, sight, or touch until we lose one of them. Our lives are balanced on our ability to utilize all of our senses. When we lose one sense the others pick up the slack. It's part of the body's perfect design and a wonderful analogy to explain the working of the body of Christ.

Spiritually speaking, we can never afford to lose our hearing. This is the true example of selective listening. It is only by our choice that we miss hearing what the Holy Spirit is telling us. How can we share a message if we do not hear it? We can communicate what we receive through our physical and spiritual senses, but hearing in our spirit is essential when it comes to relating God's message of love.

When we hear the Holy Spirit nudge us to reach out, we don't have to fear. Our handicaps are covered by God's presence in us. Once we have heard from Him, we are ready to communicate it. We use our senses and our gifts in words of love. If we answer the call to love, He will fill in where we lack, in words, talents, and desire.

Turn up your spiritual ear and hear His call to love today.

In the Stillness

Let all that I am wait quietly before God,
for my hope is in him.
PSALM 62:5 NLT

Silence. Why is it so elusive, and where do we go to find it? Could it be we aren't seeking it?

Our world is filled with perpetual noise. Each century since creation has birthed new noisemakers. We tuned into those sounds from the moment of birth. The chatter of voices, the whirling of kitchen appliances, the blare of a car horn, or tunes from the radio all compete with silence for our attention. Silence seldom wins.

Yet it is in the silence that we obtain the most and best of sounds. The gentle voice of God whispers to us in the quiet of our minds. The melodies of long-forgotten worship ring from the deep recesses of our memories when there is no other noise to drown them out. In the silence we can shut down the clamor of our racing thoughts. It's in this silence we find rest and peace.

The correlation between silence and how we function as a Christian is very important. In the stillness God speaks and shares His heart. As we listen and experience a union without the distraction of noise, He tells us the secret things that provide strength and purpose. The urge to fill in with our lists of needs and wants must be tempered if we want to bathe in His word for us.

In these times of meditation we gather the insight we need to effectively communicate the love of God to those in our circle of influence. We fill our hearts with the kind of love that doesn't require words. Then we share it with a touch, a smile, or a kind deed. Born from silence, that kind of love is true.

Love's True Expression

---

*"By this everyone will know that you
are my disciples, if you love one another."*

JOHN 13:35 NIV

Have you ever watched a mime perform? Their fluid movements and expressive faces tell a story without words. We stand in awe of the effort it takes to resist speaking. To relay a message or share a sentiment using only action is a challenge most humans would fail. We depend on language to support everything we do and feel. Only those who have had this ability taken from them can understand it's depth of usefulness.

Mimes have to think carefully about how to express their story. They might be trying to make you laugh or cry, but you will only have the benefit of physical motions to decipher which one. This kind of performance is effective because it creates pictures in your mind. Words may fade or be forgotten after an encounter, but the picture of someone or something will be embedded in your memory.

So it is with the language of love. The things we do for others will be remembered long after the words have faded into the air. Our very presence is often the thing someone needs to feel loved in that moment. We offer ourselves as companions, helpers, sisters, and friends not only for the words we might speak, but for the gift of our participation in their lives.

Just as children can sense the love of their mothers, who stroke a forehead or blow a kiss, we, too, can sense the warmth and caring from another human being that words may not express. After we have been blessed by these gifts, we are bound by love to do the same for someone else.

The expression of love continues from one to another.

What's on Your Heart?

Above all else, guard your heart,
for everything you do flows from it.
PROVERBS 4:23 NIV

We could talk forever and never exhaust the subject of God's love. Volumes of words have been written on the complexities of understanding Him, and the airwaves are full of songs of praise to Him. Since the first stone tablets to the modern-day Internet, God's virtue and wonder have been debated for all to read. He will always be sought, and some will look to His followers to see His likeness.

So many versions of the Bible exist; it would fill our bookshelves to own them all. Yet, we still keep writing about our wondrous, marvelous, and mysterious Creator. We could write into eternity and not reach the end of our search for words to express our love for Him and His great love for us. Our understanding seems to fall short. How we wish we knew it all right now and had the answers to all of life's questions.

To explain Him we must look within our hearts to find His likeness. To explain ourselves we must look upward to our Creator. Either way we must search for a tangible way to share what we know about Him and our relationship with Him. There are so many who need the message, and we must equip ourselves to tell it. Reading books about Him is not enough. We are to be extensions of the words in order to touch the world with the light of Christ.

Lean on what is written on your heart. The words God has composed there are the sentiments you need to live the life He designed for you.

You Can Believe It

And you yourself must be an example to them by doing good works of every kind. Let everything you do reflect the integrity and seriousness of your teaching.

Titus 2:7 nlt

Everyone loves a sincere person. That friend or sister who always tells the truth and seems genuine in every way. We feel comfortable and at ease with this person because we trust what they say and do. We all want to be known as a sincere person as it somehow sets us above the ordinary. People might be drawn to you when you are marked as honest and straightforward.

It's a big responsibility to carry that label. When they are very young, our children believe everything we say on faith. They aren't experienced in discerning truth and lies. Yet they want to be believed just as adults are. Even though they have not earned Mom's trust, it's natural for a child to assume she will go along with any proclamation they conjure up. After all, if Mom believes it, it must be true and right.

Ah, if only we could believe things into existence. We would have no trouble with decisions, because we could create the scenario we need, eliminating choice. There would be no situational black or white, because we could choose to believe our own assessment and make it a reality. We would be sincere because we willed it into being.

Back in the real world, it's business as usual. Sincerity is still a matter of choice, but it also demands proof. If we love as we say we love, we will prove it by the way we speak and live. Only with the right combination of God's character mixed with our outward expressions will we be deemed worthy of the trust of others.

With God's help we can make it so.

New Growth

"He cuts off every branch in me that bears no fruit,
while every branch that does bear fruit he
prunes so that it will be even more fruitful."

JOHN 15:2 NIV

Spring is a season that gives us many reminders
of God's miraculous work in our lives. Our hearts
brighten with the sights and smells of new growth and
blooming trees and flowers. Wet earth reminds us of
life-giving rains, singing birds tell the happy story of
longer days and warmer nights.

It's also the season for cleaning and pruning. The
old leaves that cover the corners of the lawn must be
gathered, and bushes and trees must be cut back to
reveal their true beauty. That birch or poplar tree in
your yard may need to have some branches removed.
Cutting away the overgrowth or useless branches will
stimulate new growth and allow for a more attractive
shape.

As with the rituals of spring, a little pruning in our lives can reveal new growth. As we cut off the branches and twigs that hide the core of who we are, we can show off our true beauty—the love of Christ in us. His love is like the center of the tree, rooted firmly, deep in the rich soil of His character.

Without all the distracting overgrowth, God's love in us becomes the center of attention. As we shed all the things that cover the best part of us, we are free to declare the reason we exist. We are a sincere representation of the living God, attracting anyone whose heart is open to experience the spring of their life. For this reason we should welcome the pruning of the Master Gardner.

Set aside all the distractions that keep others from seeing God's love in you.

A Distorted Reflection

*So all of us who have had that veil removed can see
and reflect the glory of the Lord. And the Lord—
who is the Spirit—makes us more and more like
him as we are changed into his glorious image.*

2 Corinthians 3:18 nlt

When you were a child you may have gone to a circus
and visited one of the popular sideshows, the house
of mirrors. You would stand in the midst of them,
each mirror giving you a different distorted view of
your body. Some made you look tall and thin. Some
reflected back a twisted image or one that made your
face puffy and clown-like. It was great fun to see what
you looked like in mirror after mirror.

Now that we are grown women, the images we see
in the department store dressing rooms often remind
us of the distorted reflections of that house of mirrors.
We wonder how we could possibly be what we see star-
ing back at us. It's not how you want the world to see
you. It doesn't reflect the real you.

So it is with the overriding impressions we give to those around us concerning our love for them. Inside we may have genuine feelings of affection, admiration, and respect. But outside, only our flesh shows. Our demeanor and behavior are what others see. Our words and attitudes may distort our true feelings and turn away our sisters in Christ, as well as the acquaintances we want to reach. The image we truly want to reflect, the love we sincerely want to show, is overshadowed by other things. We struggle to match the inside with the outside.

Only when we allow the Holy Spirit to balance us will we be the true image of Christ, a true reflection of love. God will make beauty of a distorted reflection, for your good and for His glory.

Step away from the mirror.

Wisdom is knowledge applied.
Head knowledge is useless on the battlefield.
Knowledge stamped on the heart makes one wise.

BETH MOORE

Effective Wisdom

Restored Communion

<hr />

If I have the gift of prophecy and can fathom all mysteries
and all knowledge, and if I have a faith that can move
mountains, but do not have love, I am nothing.

1 CORINTHIANS 13:2 NIV

Walking in a garden with God must have been a serene
experience for Eve. The sweet breezes and fragrant
flowers must have soothed her soul. Conversing with
the Creator was only possible because of her innocence
and trust in Him. She wanted for nothing and didn't
need to know anything but the love of the Father. It
was a perfect package.

As soon as she and Adam sinned, the knowledge
they gained separated them from the One whose love
they took for granted. Ever since that time humankind
has searched to replace the love and life they extinguished.
Knowledge was not a satisfactory substitute. The all-
consuming need to know left Eve with an emptiness
she could never have dreamed possible.

In the garden, communion was all they needed—not faith, not power, and not words. Now communion, and even love, was not easily obtained. All the wisdom and knowledge they gained was worth nothing in the process of building back a relationship with God. Imagine Eve's deep sense of loss and shame after her short moment of self-exultation.

You have the same opportunity as Eve each and every day. Wandering from the love of God in order to gain personal knowledge is below our calling. But His arms stretch wide to show us the mysteries we still have to discover. With communion restored, we are able to effectively extend His love. The knowledge we now have is coupled with His love to springboard us to successfully living in the center of His will.

Make It Work

For I can do everything through Christ,
who gives me strength.
PHILIPPIANS 4:13 NLT

Putting all your gifts, talents, duties, and ministries together in a way that elevates the love of Christ to the world is a daunting task. You may have powerful influence over someone or a group of people, and you may have important responsibilities in your family, job, or church. God might be using you to do great things for Him, even in small circles. But does the love factor become lost in the shuffle of progress?

It could be that you have forgotten to continually infuse the main element, the glue that holds all those things together to make the impact your heart desires, the strength of Christ. Without it you are working on your own steam.

We can't leave out the puzzle piece that makes everything else work in our lives. Certainly we can do all He asks us to do, but without the strength of Christ, our cup of love empties too quickly. Then all the "things" we do, and the way we do them, seem empty and tiring. The very ones we long to minister to miss the love factor no matter how significant our offering is to them.

Lay down your basket of spiritual goodies and seek the strength of Christ. This is how you find the love and joy you need to carry on with your calling. How refreshing it is to feel Him replenish all you lack so you can carry out His will. His strength will put power behind your love for others. Then your faith will be plentiful and your gifts a double blessing.

What's Missing?

---•◦•---

Be devoted to one another in love.
Honor one another above yourselves.
ROMANS 12:10 NIV

"But did you love them?" Their expressions stilled. She had asked the difficult question of the two missionaries sitting across the table. After hearing the long catalog of kindnesses rejected by the people they had come to bless, she had to ask, "Did you love them?"

It was a question that burned in her own heart regarding years of service that often seemed fruitless. She could relate to the couple in front of her as they continued sharing the disappointment of empty toil on the behalf of these people. Hadn't God sent them to minister? Didn't they do all they could for them, and receive in return nothing but indifference? It was as if they knew her struggle with frustration over limited results despite large faith and a willing heart.

The couple could not answer yes to her question, and she decided not to ask again. Her answer would have to be the same—no. No. This was the key none of them had possessed. Love. Love was the key that would have unlocked the power of their faith and opened doors of acceptance that eluded them.

As you think of all the times your deeds, however overflowing with faith and courage, seemed to fail to reach others, you might be tempted to give up. But the love that binds all your efforts and faith together is available to you. You don't have to conjure it up from your own well of feelings. God endows us with His precious gift of love. It's ours for the asking, and ours to give.

God's Secrets

---

*"Call to me and I will answer you and tell you
great and unsearchable things you do not know."*

Jeremiah 33:3 niv

Many of God's children have gone their own way, living life as if they knew all they needed to know. Some end up in more trouble than others, but all miss the opportunity to learn the great secrets of the universe. There is so much unknown yet to be discovered, and we serve a God who wants to share His secrets with us. Yet so many of us think we have enough knowledge to make drastic decisions, and enough love to pour into the lives of others.

It's no wonder we are ineffectual when it comes to guiding another along in the faith. We don't consider the possibility that God has more to reveal to us, and to them. Or could it be we are afraid we won't be able to assimilate the secrets of His heart, or apply them to our meager lives? Are we ready for the love and knowledge He longs to share with us?

Think of the landscape of your world. The view may be blocked by tall trees or buildings. You may not be able to see the horizon from where you stand. You know it's there, you just can't reach it from where you are. You may be familiar with the road that takes you there, but the horizon still calls to you from far away.

Now picture the landscape view from the top of a skyscraper. You can see the path to any destination and even to the horizon beyond. This is what the secrets of God do for us and in the lives of those we want to reach. All we must do is call to Him. He promises to answer and point the way. What a wonderful exchange.

Love Makes It Real

———— ✦ ————

*Love from the center of
who you are; don't fake it.*
ROMANS 12:9 MSG

It's difficult to picture the heart of a person, her true personality. Looking in a mirror only reflects the skin and features of a human, not her core being. Consequently we don't know when someone is revealing her true self or playing a game of hide-and-seek with the world.

The principles of spiritual anatomy are much the same as those in nature. The center of an apple is where life begins for the fruit. The fruit grows from the inside out. The life-bearing seeds on the inside are protected by thick fruit-meat, then by a pretty layer of skin. You can't see the seeds on the inside until you slice the fruit open. Even though the outside is attractive and sweet, the inside is what truly holds the fruit DNA we need to identify it. Only when the apple is cut open and the seeds are revealed and planted can it be truly useful.

We, too, have a rich center of seeds. Seeds for growing new faith, knowledge, and love. But they will bear new fruit only when planted in the nutrient-filled soil God has provided in other people who are ready to receive your love and expect it to be real. Faking will only betray their trust in you and shake their confidence in the things of God.

Even though we feel exposed, we must be willing to be opened up. We have opportunities to be real and let our core, Christ Jesus, be a light to the world. By the power of His love, we can stop faking and enjoy a new way of loving.

What Mountain?

Share each other's burdens,
and in this way obey the law of Christ.
GALATIANS 6:2 NLT

Depending on what part of the country you are from, mountains are described differently. In some areas of Texas a bump in the road is the only increase of elevation. But on a drive across the Northwest Cascades, the enormous jagged peaks reach to the clouds. In Switzerland, the snow-covered mountains are steep and dangerous.

Your personal mountain may seem like a giant to you, but to another it may seem like a molehill. Your perspective is shaped by your understanding of the situation and how equipped you are at the moment to climb it.

The everyday challenges of being a wife, mother, sister, and aunt are manageable some days. You have the knowledge you need to do the job and scale the interruptions on your horizon. Other days it takes all the faith you can muster to start the trek up the side of the landscape. You may even be called on to climb a mountain for a loved one or friend. This is the true test of love.

Armed with confidence, willingness, and an instruction book, you are determined to conquer or even remove that obstruction. And you may succeed. But what of the outcome? Have you simply eliminated one problem to make room for another? You might have if you left grace and charity out of the equation. Only what's done in love will have lasting effects.

Just as chopping off a weed above the ground doesn't stop the growth at the core, moving a mountain for someone may be a wasted effort if it's not done in love. Jesus always had love and God's purpose in mind when He moved mountains in the lives of others.

We must love first, and then carefully choose our mountains.

Finding Faith

———— ⋅❈⋅ ————

*For in Christ Jesus neither circumcision nor
uncircumcision has any value. The only thing
that counts is faith expressing itself through love.*
GALATIANS 5:6 NIV

Mary and Martha ran to Jesus. "If only You had been
here. Our brother would not have died." If only. Two
words that revealed the true strength of their faith.
They loved Jesus like a brother. They trusted Him and
believed Him to be who He said He was. But when
it came to matters of life and death, they had not yet
come face-to-face with the magnitude of belief that
was required to support their faith in His abilities. Do
you ever wonder how differently the story would have
turned out if they had been expecting Jesus to do what
He did?

The combination of love and faith is a powerful force, and put into practice together they can extend the possibilities for God to work in our lives.

Where do we find such love, such faith? We seek them in the heart of our Creator, who has dominion over life and death. He has fashioned us in His image and given us access to His heart, which is filled with the attributes we need to facilitate His work. We need only to ask, and He will give us all He has and is.

Loving Jesus wasn't enough for Mary and Martha, and faith alone wasn't enough for Jesus. The power to raise Lazarus came from Jesus' motivation of love and trust in the Father to do the miracle.

How might your life's story proceed if you were to find the kind of faith Jesus had? You just might find yourself raising the dead things in your life that need to live again. Faith must be found. It's not hiding, just waiting, ready for you to tap in.

It Feels Like Love

And whatever you do, whether in word or deed,
do it all in the name of the Lord Jesus,
giving thanks to God the Father through him.
COLOSSIANS 3:17 NIV

As the room came into focus the little girl cried,
forgetting where she was and why her head throbbed.
A nurse approached the bed and patted her shoulder.
"Are you waking up?" she asked cheerfully. The little
girl whimpered but could not speak. Slowly, her vision
cleared. She reached for whatever was scratching her
left eye, but the nurse grabbed her hand. Then she
tucked something under the girl's arm and wiped away
the tears dripping from her chin.

"Honey, you can't touch your eye. It's covered in a
patch. But here is your teddy, and he has a patch, too."
Happy to see her bear, she felt the patch. The nurse
held up a mirror to the little girl's face. "See, he looks
just like you."

You have probably been the recipient of an act of kindness at least once in your life. And if you were a child at the time, it may have felt very much like an act of love. Even the smallest gestures can make the difference between joy and despair. The impression these moments make in the life of another are eternal, and may spread beyond your scope of influence.

Love in the general sense, love for your fellow man, makes strong medicine. Whether you call it grace, affection, kindness, or generosity, it has the same healing, ministering effect. Knowing what someone needs and making it happen, no matter how inconvenient, is the expression of God's love so needed in the world today.

Is there someone in your life who needs a teddy bear?

Time Wasted

But seek first his kingdom and his righteousness,
and all these things will be given to you as well.
MATTHEW 6:33 NIV

Running a house and raising children are time-consuming occupations. Whether you are organized or operate haphazardly, it's hard work. The résumé of responsibilities has changed over the years, and the temptation to take on more and more is often fed by peer pressure and self-imposed expectations.

You may find yourself under a mound of duties that are neither satisfying nor gainful. The reality is that many of the things we do in life are a waste of our time, and more importantly, a waste of God's precious time. There are activities we could lay down to make way for more constructive commitments.

God asks us to search our motives for all we do. Painful as it may be, He also asks us to cut away at the busyness that distracts us from what He has called us to do. Even though the praised Proverbs 31 woman modeled what some deem perfection in womanhood, she, too, may have neglected a call on her life to simply love. Busyness does not equal ministry. Order does not equal righteousness. But these are the traps that keep us from our call to love.

The commandments we find in the Bible to love far outnumber any scriptures on organization and perpetual service. Only what we do in love is worthy of praise. Our efforts are matched by God tenfold when they're bathed in love for Him and His children.

Thanks to our partnership with Him we are more effective in His kingdom. His love covers all we do and stretches our time so we can accomplish His design for us.

*He broke the life of His own Son to redeem
us and now He wants to use our lives
as a sacrament to nourish others.*

OSWALD CHAMBERS, *CONFORMED TO HIS IMAGE*

Sincere Sacrifice

The Real Gift

If I give all I possess to the poor and give
over my body to hardship that I may boast,
but do not have love, I gain nothing.

1 CORINTHIANS 13:3 NIV

Who doesn't love receiving a gift? Packages and ribbons and the delight of the unknown are pleasures we all enjoy. For some, giving is more satisfying. You may have someone in your life who gives away possessions to anyone who admires them. Grandmothers and aunts are often ones to share their trinkets, quilts, and linens. And some will give away anything just to make sure others aren't in need.

Self-imposed pressure to offer up more than you have to give is not the example God would have you follow. The desire to be satisfied by your generosity lacks the one element that makes giving effective. Love. Without it, all your efforts will leave you feeling empty. It seems as though you have fallen short of your goal.

Giving is often no more than a social exchange or an obligation met. But in the likeness of Jesus, giving is the reflection of His sacrifice for us. Our motives separate genuine sacrifice from shallow efforts to appease others. We know what His motivation was, and we can follow His design for the best kind of gift giving.

The truest gift you can give anyone is the love of Jesus. Even better is when it's passed through your heart, your core being. Toil and busyness to the point of physical exhaustion doesn't mean you have loved today; it only means you have played the game we all play from time to time. The game of false sacrifice.

Ask God today what His heart is on the subject of giving. His way is a better way.

What's in It for Me?

Humble yourselves, therefore,
under God's mighty hand,
that he may lift you up in due time.
1 Peter 5:6 NIV

You've worked hard on a project or event for your church or friends. You gave up a lot of time and energy to do your part and even stepped in when others failed to do theirs. You listened to criticism and heard others take credit for your work. It's heartbreaking to see that you are unappreciated, and you feel used.

"But, God," you say, "I worked so hard and no one cares."

Welcome to the human race. We are constantly seeking approval and gratitude for the great sacrifices we have made for others. When it doesn't come, we find ways to glorify our fine contribution to the world, the church, or our homes. We go on "fishing" expeditions to draw out compliments and praise. It seldom works, and we are eventually either embarrassed or put in our place.

When it comes to sacrifice or service, humility is the answer. If we are serving from the heart with an attitude of love, not expecting anything in return, we are free to enjoy the experience. Letting go of the need for approval will give God the opportunity to exalt you in His way and in His time.

This is the best kind of promotion. You will never have to worry about praise if you stop asking what's in it for you. How pleased God will be to see you seek only His will in your sacrifice. He can use you to the fullest if you are not focused on yourself, but on the power of service through charity.

How Much Is Enough?

***

"But he knows the way that I take;
when he has tested me, I will come forth as gold."
JOB 23:10 NIV

When we think of a biblical character who lost everything, Job certainly comes to mind. This obscure person's experience was so profound it warranted its own book in the Old Testament. If you have found it difficult to read, you're not alone. Job's story of suffering and hardship, while not typical of the kind of agony we go through in our lives, does strike a painful chord in our hearts.

You have no doubt had a taste of Job's suffering. As a woman you have invested energy and emotion in raising children and building relationships with friends and family. Sometimes your sacrifice has turned to suffering. When life gets out of control, you may have asked some of the same questions of God that Job did. And finally you echo Job's sentiment—enough!

Sacrifice in times of plenty is easy. Sacrifice in the midst of turmoil is not usually our first choice of action. Our love for God, our spouse, our children, and our friends can be challenged just as Job's was challenged. But love must win out. When we cling to love as if it were our only hope, love cradles us until we are able to praise God in our circumstances.

Perhaps like Job you have lost a child or been overwhelmed with friends who just don't understand. You have questioned yourself and God and are ready to say "enough." This is the place God can pour out His mercy and love. Now you will understand the soothing balm of love and apply it when others need it.

Surrender your suffering to Jesus and He will turn it into profit for your life.

Compared to Christ

---

*God can pour on the blessings in astonishing ways
so that you're ready for anything and everything,
more than just ready to do what needs to be done.*

2 CORINTHIANS 9:8 MSG

You've heard it many times—"you can't outgive God."
We know in our heart this is true. None of us could
give the gift of eternal life, or any of the blessings that
God gives. We come from a different place than God
when it comes to giving.

God gives from the abundance of the love He has
for us. This love supersedes anything we could do for
another human. The gift of His son was the gift to
top all gifts. Compared to Him, we fall short. But as
Christians, the call to give is still ours. We have been
blessed beyond measure and we are asked to bless in
return. The cost may be great, but the rewards are
equally great.

Christ gave freely out of an obedient heart. He gave out of love and for love's sake, willingly and freely. So we are also to give out of love, freely, and not to be sad about it. When we remember the gift we have been given, how can we give begrudgingly? We are not forced to; it is an expectation that flows from knowing the necessity of generosity and benevolence.

God knows we are reluctant to sacrifice—it's a result of our self-centered nature. As we take on the humility of Christ's sacrifice, giving becomes a natural tendency. We can never repay our debt, but we can carry on the spirit of love by giving with a heart of gratitude. Then He will surprise you by supplying all your needs and then some.

Behind the Smile

———— ◆◆◆ ————

God is not a man, so he does not lie.

NUMBERS 23:19 NLT

There is no mystery about God's ways. He is what He says He is and never needs to boast. Everything He does is for good, without any motives that would make us question Him. There is no "shadow of turning" with Him or His ways. When He gives, it's out of mercy and grace, unlike our limited generosity.

So many people within our reach are needy. We are faced with choices every day to either help meet their needs or walk away. Even though we appear to be on top of the giving game, there are times when we can't make it happen.

Some days it's hard to stay filled with the sentiments we want to have toward others. We go through the motions, submitting to the plans of others. But behind the smile, we feel no urge to be inconvenienced by their needs, no matter how great they may be. So we smile and do our duty to give, even though it's not truthful in spirit.

God's grace covers you. He knows you have times when your own needs prevent you from engaging in the flow of loving acts. When you can be honest with Him about your struggle to pour out to someone else, He will provide the love you lack. His greatest desire is to see you in tune with Him in ministry, not conjuring up a smile, a feeling, or an act of generosity out of a sense of duty.

Let Him be the force behind all you do.

It's Not Mine

"When someone has been given much, much will be required in return; and when someone has been entrusted with much, even more will be required."

LUKE 12:48 NLT

The boy wore a determined look as he told his father he was running away from home. Wise enough to see an opportunity to teach, the father told him that he would be missed, but if that's what he felt he had to do, then he was free to go.

Surprised, the boy surveyed his bedroom and picked up his backpack. He grabbed a few things from his dresser and stuffed them in the pack.

"I'm sorry, son, but those things don't belong to you. I bought them. You will have to do without those." The boy glared at his father and threw the items on the floor. After some deliberation he grabbed his prized new basketball shoes.

"Son, you only paid for half of that pair of shoes, so please leave the one I bought."

After several minutes of the banter, the boy gave up and left home with nothing—only to return in repentance that evening.

God has provided all our needs and many of our wants. But considering that God is the creator of all things, we must realize that what we think we possess doesn't belong to us. They are only on loan from Him, and He entrusts them to us while there is life on earth. As we take inventory of our possessions, gifts, and talents, we must consider where to invest them. They were meant to bless us and are all part of His plan to bless someone else as well.

By sharing what you have been given with the same love He showed you, the blessing lasts twice as long.

What Matters Most?

And since we are his children, we are his heirs.
In fact, together with Christ we are heirs of
God's glory. But if we are to share his glory,
we must also share his suffering.

ROMANS 8:17 NLT

The journey from glory to suffering is one we take with
great anticipation and with great trepidation. Everyone
must discover which path to take, the one that God
has planned for them. The divine lessons we learn
along the way serve to knit us together with Him. He
may gently guide or give a resounding "this way!" to
direct us.

If you could see very far ahead on this journey, you
might wish you could abandon it. Sharing the high
points along the way is exciting and encouraging, but
the suffering down the road is not as appealing.

Your suffering is tempered by His protective arm and His overflowing mercy. This is what comes from being heirs of God. This is the gift that keeps you moving when the road is rough, the gift you give away to others to demonstrate God's love.

What might your suffering look like, and would you have suffered anyway? There are many in this world who suffer great tragedies, all the while giving God the glory for His goodness to them. They have come to understand that the ultimate purpose in their suffering is to eventually ease the pain of someone else. Sharing someone else's suffering is a sacrifice that requires understanding.

You may have shared in the glory already, or you may still be suffering. Wherever you are in your journey, let the inspiration of God's loving care be a roadmap to your ultimate destination. Then share His glory with those whose lives He has entrusted you to touch.

Tall Tales

—— ◆ ——

I have no interest in giving you a chatty account of my adventures, only the wondrously powerful and transformingly present words and deeds of Christ in me that triggered a believing response among the outsiders.

Romans 15:18 MSG

As adult women we are free to do what we like. The more decisions we make on our own, the less we need someone to help us make them. The freedom is a gift, but with freedom sometimes comes pride, and with pride sometimes comes false humility, because pride and true humility don't mix.

Even though women often struggle with low self-esteem, our nature is not inclined to choose humility. We may unknowingly begin the habit of generating counterfeit humility instead of genuinely putting on the cloak of a humble servant. We choose the sacrifices that are easy but will make us look good. We have chosen to deceive ourselves and believe God and others are likewise fooled. It's not that we are bad people, just not sold out to the true sacrifices. We are not willing to give up any credit for what we do.

If this is why you boast, there is nothing to boast about. Anytime you steal God's glory for yourself it's an empty sacrifice. But when you find yourself serving and giving without thought of any personal gain or praise, you have found a new freedom.

What a relief not to be tethered to the spotlight. What a joy to see the glory going to the One who deserves it. We partake of this glory by letting go of the need to be recognized. It's always a win-win with God.

The Eternal Element

Trust GOD from the bottom of your heart;
don't try to figure out everything on your own.
Listen for GOD's voice in everything you do,
everywhere you go; he's the one who will keep you on track.

PROVERBS 3:5–6 MSG

We hold certain things precious—our children's happiness, financial security, our homes. But what are these to gain for us? We are short-sighted when it comes to seeking gain, attempting to extract it from people or things that are temporal.

Eternal gain should be our goal, but the issue that confronts us daily is where to find eternal thinking. We cannot rely on our own judgment, our own choices, or our own voice. The only way to know how to make sacrifice work for the gain of the kingdom is to look to God. He is the light unto our path that illuminates the instructions and mentality we need to proceed in giving and serving.

This is how we fit into the program of God's plan for the world. We listen and put on charity before we ever take a step. When we are ready to see sacrifice in the light of eternity, we know we have embraced God's heart. The things we hold precious are often the very things that need to take second place in our lives, second place to eternity.

As you walk through your day, trying to make everything come out even, take time to enlarge your perspective to include His vision. You might find that your efforts to give unselfishly do not carry the weight of God's touch. If His fingerprints are not on what you do for others, you may be missing the eternal element. Lean only on His way of thinking and you will begin to minister as you never have before.

Do It Afraid

For God has not given us a spirit of fear and timidity,
but of power, love, and self-discipline.

2 TIMOTHY 1:7 NLT

She stepped through the soup kitchen door. Her heart pounded with fear of the unknown. Although her greatest desire was to reach out and help those less fortunate than herself, she was in unfamiliar territory and unsure of her resolve. Had she really heard from God about coming here, or was this just an effort to satisfy some sort of need for His approval and praise?

We have all been here, fearful to leave our comfort zone and sacrifice our vulnerability for the cause of Christ. This has stopped many Christians from moving beyond their perceived abilities and venturing into territory that would bless them. They miss the opportunity to bring glory to God in ways they couldn't have imagined. For some, risks are nothing to worry about.

But for most of us, placing ourselves in a sacrificial position is difficult and scary. We resist the nudge and lose out on the blessing.

You must step out in faith, even if you have to do it afraid. God is not going to lead you into any situation that He hasn't prepared for you in advance. This is your confidence when it comes to reaching out and going where He has called you. Your strength, wisdom, and courage come from Him. But more importantly, go when you are padded with His gift of charity. This is not only for your protection, but for the ministry you are called to do each and every day.

Whether it's a soup kitchen, church women's tea, or trip to an impoverished country, when we are armed with the love of God, we need not fear. Through God's power there is joy in sacrifice.

Love recognizes no barriers. It jumps hurdles,
leaps fences, penetrates walls to arrive
at its destination full of hope.

Maya Angelou

Portrait of Love

Love Looks Like God

Love is patient, love is kind. It does not envy,
it does not boast, it is not proud. It does not
dishonor others, it is not self-seeking, it is not
easily angered, it keeps no record of wrongs.

1 CORINTHIANS 13:4–5 NIV

The childlike faith in parents, the wet kisses of a kitten, the old man stooping to caress his dying wife. These are images that bring to mind the question, is this love? Our souls are always searching for love's meaning and longing for its fullness. But we have been given the wrong impression about what love really looks like.

The media would have us believe love is a passionate drive to own someone else. Literature has attempted to write about it down through the centuries without a definitive conclusion. Our mouths speak the word *love* as if it applies to anything that brings us pleasure.

You may wonder what the portrait of love would look like if God painted it. He has told us in words what love is *not* through this verse in 1 Corinthians 13. If we close our eyes and try to imagine the picture He paints there, we could fashion it into the image that suits us. It would be as abstract as a portrait we might paint of God. The more we fellowship with Him, the more we see Him. The more we practice love as He paints it, the more intimately we share it.

When we read this scripture we are reminded how much we need God who *is* love to make sense of it all. We all think the same thing when reading this chapter: how will I ever live up to this picture of love? We will do it through the strength of God living in us.

What a wonderful gift God has given us—Himself. It's what love looks like.

Lay It Down

My dear brothers and sisters, take note of this:
Everyone should be quick to listen, slow to speak
and slow to become angry, because human anger
does not produce the righteousness that God desires.

JAMES 1:19–20 NIV

We live in a world of injustice, cruelty, and evil. But when anger grips our hearts, it's seldom due to these universal offenses. More often our anger stems from a personal hurt or something we think is unfair. When we don't get our way, we are angry. When our plans are cut short, our blood boils. Anger can affect everything we do and say. And it can make fools out of normally sound individuals.

If we are dedicated to preserving the character of God in us, we cannot tarnish His reputation with anger and its consequences. There is no room for human anger in the union of spirit and flesh. When we are continually angry, it is often because we believe we have rights. But we have none. When we die to self and put on the righteousness of Christ, He will be our defender and protector. His ways are higher and in perfect order, without strife.

To allow anger to seep into the temple of the Most High God, our very own bodies, is giving the enemy of our souls a chance to take up residence. He will use our anger to destroy our message of love to the world, discrediting all we have worked to accomplish. As a result, we are let down and discouraged. God wants so much more for us than the isolation negative emotions create.

You can't hide an angry countenance. It doesn't draw anyone to you or make your acts of love believable. Don't jeopardize your Christlike integrity. Lay down your rights today.

Let It Go

Be generous with the different things God gave you,
passing them around so all get in on it: if words,
let it be God's words; if help, let it be God's hearty help.

1 PETER 4:10 MSG

The path between your agenda and God's is riddled with potholes and pit stops. This is especially true for relationships. You were created with a need for intimacy, and your desire for close friendships is evidence of God's design.

If only we would follow His plan instead of our own when it comes to loving and serving others. While our nature is self-serving and short sighted, God's nature is to love and serve first, for He sees the bigger picture of each person's destiny. Although we need not help God along, we can be an important part of shaping the destiny of another if we will only let go of our agenda.

Sometimes we are nervous about extending ourselves beyond our immediate clan. The people closest to us are priority, but we are still called to reach out in fellowship. When we neglect those opportunities because of fear or apathy, that is also self-serving, and it's not an expression of the love God wants to plant in us. He wants to use us to bring about miracles in the lives of friends, family, and even strangers. This is the equation of perfection in service—His love in us plus His agenda.

When you open up your heart and mind to new paths and new ways of reaching out, God will guide you to specific people you are to love in a tangible way.

Remember Not

━━━ ◆ ━━━

Make allowance for each other's faults,
and forgive anyone who offends you. Remember,
the Lord forgave you, so you must forgive others.

COLOSSIANS 3:13 NLT

There should be a flower named *Remember Not*. *Forget Me Not* is a sweet sentiment and a reminder of love's expression, but it suggests that the remembrances would be nice ones. If only our memories were more selective in a positive way. Wouldn't it be wonderful to remember only the good in people and not remember all the bad? Our marriages would be bolstered and our example to our children would be exemplary, for it's the kind, loving act that covers all sins and mirrors God's love for us. He is the judge of all sins, and though we do not excuse all bad behavior, we need not take on the responsibility of tracking them.

Keeping track of wrongs against you is a choice. If you refuse to be a scorekeeper you will have more successful relationships, choosing mercy over revenge. You will never be able to completely hide all the ill feelings painful memories cause, but remind yourself of the forgiveness given you by God and extend that forgiveness to others. Then you must choose not to count it against them anymore.

You are so blessed to serve a God that does not count your faults and mistakes against you. This is the expression of love that, although it's a challenge to live up to, encompasses the character of God in you. And even though it's the right thing to do, it's easily faked. Only you and your Creator know if you have truly thrown away your precious list of wrongs. Only He knows what is in your heart.

Remember not? It's a choice, and oh, what peace will follow.

Break Free

For wherever there is jealousy and selfish ambition,
there you will find disorder and evil of every kind.
JAMES 3:16 NLT

Her best friend stood in front of the crowd, wearing the crown she should have won. After all, she was prettier and more talented than her friend could ever be. It wasn't fair. Now someone else would receive all the attention and admiration she had wanted—she still wanted. Wearing that crown was her dream, and now she would have to show happiness for her undeserving friend. The pain inside was beginning to grow. She could barely manage a smile.

You might be saying that you would never respond that way if this were your story. You are sure you would be a gracious loser and be ecstatic for your friend. A little envy is acceptable, isn't it? Surely it would never stand in the way of a loving relationship. You would never let it go that far.

Envy is a sliver that festers in our hearts. It's one of the strongest wedges between friends, and generally an acceptable weakness. Everyone experiences envy at some time. As innocent as the emotion might seem, if not resisted it will squash love and feed all the negative feelings you may have.

The good news is that you don't have to hang on to envy. As soon as you realize it holds you hostage, you can break free with the help of the Holy Spirit. When you can see that you have exactly what God wants you to have, and more than you deserve, wanting what others have isn't so attractive.

True love rejoices in the gifts others receive, as if you had given them yourself.

An Uncluttered Mind

—◆◆◆—

Summing it all up, friends, I'd say you'll do best
by filling your minds and meditating on things true,
noble, reputable, authentic, compelling, gracious—
the best, not the worst; the beautiful, not the ugly;
things to praise, not things to curse.

PHILIPPIANS 4:8 MSG

There are moments in your day when you may be over-loaded with mental lists, images of unfinished projects or questions on how to accomplish a task. The noise in your thoughts distracts you from moving forward. You have taken on too many burdens and responsibilities to manage emotionally, and it feels like a huge weight on your shoulders. Now add to that all the feelings that occupy your energy such as anger, jealousy, disap-pointment, and pride.

These negative emotions press in on us throughout the day, so heavy that eventually we want to give up. The extra baggage shows in our countenance as it becomes harder to disguise. Peace and joy are elusive, and we realize how long it's been since our minds were filled with thanksgiving and praise to God.

We can blame it on the people in our lives, the circumstances of strained relationships, but we know God wants us to dwell on the things that are profitable, the things that encourage love for Him. Then we are equipped to answer His call to love without the entanglements of negativity and ill feelings.

This discipline of self-monitoring is important to our well-being and fellowship with God. It must be pleasing to Him when He can speak to us without barriers around our minds. And what a refreshing peace takes residence in our hearts when the negative noise is silenced, our ability to love enhanced. The cleansing that takes place when we refuse the confusing voices that dominate our thoughts is a relief to our souls.

Dwell on the good things God has given you.

Righteousness or Retaliation

Do to others as you would
have them do to you.
LUKE 6:31 NIV

Were you taught the Golden Rule in grade school?
Most of the kids in your class probably didn't know
it was from the Bible. It was one of those sayings that
school teachers used to control behavior or Sunday
school teachers used to remind us that God was watching us.

Regardless of what we thought as a child, the
Golden Rule remains a standard for the way we treat
others. It's the right thing to do, treat others as you
want to be treated. A simplistic rule for a difficult
practice. Our selfish nature is more inclined to retaliate
when someone criticizes or treats us poorly. But God
calls us to righteousness in our response and in our
actions.

We desire our children to live by the golden rule, not only for the benefit of others, but for reputation's sake. What parent doesn't want their child to be the model child—kind, caring, and adhering to divine and moral laws? It's a reflection on our parenting skills and the revelation to all that we have the perfect child! It's a selfish way to think.

But God also wants His children to live righteous lives, showing kindness and love to all. He wants us to reflect His character and show the world that we are operating under the rules of love's expression. Giving more than we take, an act of kindness or a prayer said for another is much more productive than retaliation of any sort.

As we teach our children that kindness and following the Golden Rule is more than politeness, they will look for our example. When we can live it out they will see it's pleasing to God, the way to secure a relationship and spread the message of God's unfailing love.

Wait for God

———— ✦ ————

*Wait for the LORD; be strong
and take heart and wait for the LORD.*

PSALM 27:14 NIV

When we are in a benevolent mood, that moment in time when we desire to reach out, our impulse may be misguided. There is a time to jump into a friendship and there is a time when God may say, "No, wait." His viewpoint is our guide. His wisdom is our standard. We make big decisions only after requesting His approval. We must also look to Him before we volunteer for what we think are small concerns.

While God's love doesn't entertain selection or exclusion when given, He knows who is best suited to befriend or mentor certain ones. The best fit is known only to the Creator. He cares about every exchange between His children. We tend to believe ourselves to be appropriate for any person at any time. But we should consider God's matchmaking in the light of His will for us.

Immersion in the love of God doesn't automatically make us universally ready for all relationships. We must first take time to pray and ask for discernment for where we are best used, and who we are best suited to build a loving relationship with. This is a better way to love, following the design and choosing who God chooses for us. This is true not just for romantic relationships; it should be a pattern we use for all.

Take a moment today and pray for God to bring the people He has chosen into your life, and for you to be the right person to demonstrate God's love to them. This is a better approach to perfection in love.

Picture This

But anyone who does not love
does not know God, for God is love.

1 JOHN 4:8 NLT

On the wall of his bedroom hung a picture of the ocean. The scene included a sailing ship with a tall mast and sails billowing in the wind. Each night he stared at the painting, dreaming of one day seeing the ocean and sailing on a giant windjammer. As he drifted off to sleep he could imagine the salty breeze and the waves splashing against the bow.

One day the boy's father took him to the ocean. The ships he saw were enormous, rusty steam vessels packed with cargo. Row upon row of boats lined the harbor. None had sails or masts. The boy was confused.

"Father, where are the real boats?"

The painting of love that hangs on the walls of your mind may not be a true representation of it. We set our hearts on what is familiar, what we saw as a child, or what others have told us love looks like. Then we base our methods on those impressions, wondering why our efforts are lacking.

God will paint the portrait of His love for you. He has divinely mixed colors and hues to create the perfect reflection of love, which is Himself. This is the portrait we want imprinted on our hearts and minds. Then we can feel confident in our recognition of love's true expression.

What is the picture of love you have come to know? Is familiarity enough, or will you need the Master Painter to make Himself known to you? Ask Him to reveal His love, and you will have a new picture to inspire you.

To love another person is like God, to draw them to life and to gift them with identity and significance. To love is to see the image of God in them—that unique spark of God entrusted to them—and affirm it.

Paul J. Wadell, *Becoming Friends*

I Believe in You

A Tall Order

—————•◆•—————

Love does not delight in evil but rejoices
with the truth. It always protects, always
trusts, always hopes, always perseveres.

1 CORINTHIANS 13:6–7 NIV

The attributes that these verses demand are a tall order to fill, unless we tap into the very heart of God and let His charity flow through us as we live out our lives here on earth. Protecting, trusting, and hoping are all attitudes we might freely give to our loved ones. But how hard it is to extend these to the unlovable and undeserving.

The truth is that none of us are deserving, and trying to muster up the actions described here is not well accomplished without the love of Christ in us, flowing through us. It is by our relationship with Him that we come to be a vessel. The kind of vessel we become is our choice.

Think back to when you were a child. Remember the warm feeling that came over you when your parents praised you, demonstrated hope and trust in you, or covered you with their protective arms. We still crave these feelings as adults. We feel good when someone shows appreciation for or trust in us.

As women we have the opportunity to generate encouragement to our sisters in Christ. We are especially good at building up another person. But we are also very apt at tearing down when we cut off the flow of God's character through us. Jealousy, apathy, and a competitive spirit stand in the way.

A daily choice to access charity is the way to a double blessing. The giver and the recipient will know the joy that comes from obedience to the Word, the command to love.

Rejoicing is always a more satisfying and contagious occupation.

Commitment over Feelings

Our people must learn to devote themselves
to doing what is good, in order to provide for
urgent needs and not live unproductive lives.

TITUS 3:14 NIV

The best kind of love is born from a commitment not a feeling. Feelings come and go, so we may lose our ability to love if we base it on emotion. Commitment is a choice, and it gives power to our acts of charity. Effective love does not come from overwhelming desire; it is rather a thoughtful decision.

Our commitment to be loving to others is the stable force that builds the body of Christ. We can love much deeper and more like Christ if we are not standing on the shaky foundation of feelings. We stand instead on the rock of Jesus' love. His presence in our lives supplies the affection and caring attitude others long for. We give it willingly because we hope to see increase in the lives of those we help.

You may be aware of all the hurting and wounded souls around you, but until you are willing to undertake the commission to put forth your hand in love, no matter how difficult, you will not convince anyone you are a follower of Jesus. The lost seek proof, and they know the difference between temporary, superficial gestures and true dedication to His cause.

We find strength to keep our commitments as we remember all that God committed to us while we were still sinning and lost. His choice is always to love, restore, redeem, and preserve. We will find joy and peace as we make the same pledge to serve up love to the ones who need to see Jesus.

The Other Cheek

---

*"Bless those who curse you. Pray for those
who hurt you. If someone slaps you on
one cheek, offer the other cheek also."*

LUKE 6:28–29 NLT

The difficult people in our lives require just as much or
more love than those who readily receive our affection.
God's expectation for us is the same no matter who is
set before us. Jesus taught us about those who test our
patience and benevolence. His charge to pray for and
bless those who mistreat us is indeed a challenge.

Women, whether in the workplace or at home,
are especially vulnerable to hurt feelings and provoca-
tion. We are natural born protectors, nurturers, and
organizers, and even with the best of intentions, a
spirit of competition can divide us. Feathers are ruffled
and opinions rebutted. Females are not exempt from
ego-driven words and actions, which cause challenging
attitudes to rear their heads.

Love demands death to self, even in dealing with those who we perceive to be unfair, wrong, or deceitful. Then, just as Jesus did, we are to offer forgiveness and keep on loving. Impossible? Yes, in our own strength. But there lives in us a living God with living, active love that extends to everyone. This is the strength we need to put ourselves last, just as Jesus did when dealing with less than cooperative people. When we are successful at taking on a Christlike attitude toward people who challenge us, we dare not take credit ourselves, but give thanks and glory to the One who made it possible.

Stay true to the character of God resident in your life. Do the unexpected by submitting not to evil, but to mercy and charity of heart. This is what will end any standoff and prove the love of God is alive.

Persistence in Relationships

---◆◆◆---

As iron sharpens iron,
so a friend sharpens a friend.
Proverbs 27:17 nlt

Face it. We need one another. God created in us a need
for fellowship with Him and with other human beings.
The divine purpose of relationships is complicated, yet
simple at the same time. Regardless of how many or
what kind of friends we have, it's a source of character
growth and an opportunity for showing the best kind
of love.

You probably have long-time friends in your
life who have challenged you in ways that make you
squirm. You may even want to run far away from them
at times. Irritations and hurt feelings come with the
friendship territory.

We sharpen one another in ways that are un-comfortable or require great humility. Still we cling to these friends even though we don't enjoy being sharpened. The drive to fill up the friendship hole keeps us coming back for more sharpening. Inside we know it's pleasing to God when we allow Him to add those people in our lives we need to point us to Jesus, through either pleasure or pain.

Some relationships call for persistence in love. You can choose to pursue loving your less lovable friends, or you can give up and miss what God wants to teach you through that person.

Christian friends can be the vessels God uses to bring perspective to trying times, joy to times of celebration, or prayer in times of questioning. Will you also be that friend? Will other women want to be persistent in their love for you? Don't give up too easily on others or yourself. Decide today to love the friends God has placed in your life.

More Than Tolerance

---

*Once we, too, were foolish and disobedient. We were misled
and became slaves to many lusts and pleasures. Our lives
were full of evil and envy, and we hated each other. But—
"When God our Savior revealed his kindness and love, he
saved us, not because of the righteous things we had done,
but because of his mercy. He washed away our sins, giving
us a new birth and new life through the Holy Spirit."*

TITUS 3:3–5 NLT

The words in the e-mail cut like a knife through her
heart. Someone who had been a friend was now an ad-
versary for no apparent reason. Accusations jumped off
the screen, dark and mean. She stared at them, hoping
there was some mistake. Or was this a joke?

A few months later she came face-to-face with her
accuser. Her heart pounded as she thought about how
to react. God filled her with grace, His grace. The meet-
ing went as if the harsh words were never said. It was
more than tolerance for her; it was supernatural grace.

Many times we are called upon to extend grace to those we feel don't deserve it. It is the expression of God's love that, when it comes from the Father, heals, honors, and preserves even the most strained relationships. Grace given from the reserves of our human heart is not enough to permeate the pain of sin. Grace must come from its origin, the God of forgiveness and mercy. It is by His mercy we are able to share in His grace, and it is by His grace we are able to extend mercy to others.

Mere tolerance cannot rejoice in the repair of someone's life. It cannot build up another, and it cannot protect from the effects of strife in relationships. We must have more. We must have the sincere love of the Father that covers us all.

He gives you access to this great gift. All you need to do is receive it. Then let it spill out to those you come in contact with.

Teamwork

"And if you give even a cup of cold water to one of the least of my followers, you will surely be rewarded."

MATTHEW 10:42 NLT

The marathon runner knows how to persevere. The subtle tricks to stay on track, the mind-set to motivate, and the concentration it requires to stay focused on the finish line are all tools the runner uses to win the race. Even when the body wants to surrender to the pain and torture of endurance, an experienced athlete will find the strength to reach the end.

There is flag-waving and high fives from the crowds who want him to succeed, even though they can't relate to his agony. Reaching out with cups of cool water, they join in a team effort to energize and inspire.

Fortunately, the prize he receives is not only the medal around his neck but the satisfaction of knowing he stayed the course. His crowd of supporters isn't able to share in the glory, but they have been part of his journey. They believed in his dream, even if they couldn't understand it completely.

This is what the love of God does for us. We run the race of Christianity, following Jesus in toil and in joy. We love to see people on the sidelines cheering us on. They help us stay true to the race.

What kind of cheerleader have you been at someone's race? Are you willing to assist another as they strive to stay on their feet? As you reach out with that cup of water, you will remember how many times you were refreshed and revived by another person.

Stay the course, help someone finish their race.

Am I Invisible?

Don't be selfish; don't try to impress others.
Be humble, thinking of others as better than
yourselves. Don't look out only for your own
interests, but take an interest in others too.

PHILIPPIANS 2:3–4 NLT

The ladies at her table in the retreat dining hall chattered away. They talked shop for an hour, never once noticing that she wasn't entering into the conversation. How could she? She wasn't part of their clan. So she sat in silence, eating her meal, hoping someone would ask her a question or comment on her pretty pink jacket. It was as if she were invisible.

We have all experienced this feeling at some time, or we may be one of those who never notice the outsider. Exclusion is not in Christ's vocabulary, neither should it be in ours. At the very least, we honor each other as sisters in His family. This means seeing, really seeing the person across the table.

Love does not exclude, even in mere conversation, yet it happens often even in Christian circles. There are too many egos to jump over, too many women trying to overcome their self-doubt, to let in the one who may need to be heard or seen.

God longs for us to know that He sees us. It's His desire that we never feel invisible—that isolation never takes hold of our hearts when we feel left out. We are never alone. He is our constant companion and hears every word we say. He calls for us to share our heart's cry with Him. No more shall we slip into obscurity, for He exalts us as His children.

We don't have to impress God. We can sit at His table and He will never exclude us. He sees us fully and loves us just as we are.

Bragging Rights

*Therefore encourage one another and build
each other up, just as in fact you are doing.*

1 THESSALONIANS 5:11 NIV

Who doesn't like to hear a word of praise for a job well
done? When it seems as though our efforts go unno-
ticed, we ache for a glimpse of recognition. Validation
is important to everyone and a little bit can satisfy
our aching for someone to believe in us. Even when
we know God gives the thumbs-up, a pat on the back
from our peers helps so much to affirm us. If we cannot do this for one another, then we are not fulfilling
the commission of the Father to love one another as we
love ourselves.

Our hopes for our friends should be of the highest
kind. Encouragement not only reinforces God's work
in their lives, but feeds the determination of those
wanting to use their gifts for God.

Inspiring courage and spirit in others is the stimulation they might need to persevere through doubts and insecurity. Since it invokes a feeling of significance, this act of love is not often forgotten. You may have your own memories of a teacher, a parent, or a friend who made you believe in yourself. These are the moments you look back on when doubt creeps in to keep you from your dreams.

Hope is our imitation of God's attitude toward all His children. His hope is that we will take on His character and rejoice with our fellow humans when they do their best for God. We keep on hoping against all signs of failure and against odds that loom over us. We persevere because we know that with God there are no odds. He has already ordained our path, but we need encouragement to walk it.

Encourage, rejoice with, and hope for someone today.

Be My Friend

—— ⋆ ——

"Greater love has no one than this:
to lay down one's life for one's friends."

JOHN 15:13 NIV

No one really knows how they will react in a life-and-death situation. Your convictions, personality, and fortitude would all play a part in a sudden decision to give up your life. We might say we would certainly die for someone else, but self-preservation is a strong force, and it would be impossible to predict if it would win over our desire to save another person.

Can we measure our spiritual maturity by our determination to lay down our lives? Or can we gauge our love for God by it? Maybe not, but more importantly, can we lay down our lives in a less literal sense on a daily basis? There are many moments in our interactions with our friends and loved ones where we could choose to set aside our agendas and needs. If we stay alert we will be aware of small opportunities to lay down our desires for another.

Our attitude toward loving others comes from understanding the involvement Christ has in our lives—that He already gave His life for us. When we put on Christ's cloak of humility, our priorities change. We are able to see the value of another life, and the necessity of sacrificial love.

As we determine to be faithful to the call to love one another, we must also be faithful to the call to lay down our lives, our agendas and comfort, for others. There is a special kind of joy that comes from this act of obedience.

No Matter How Long

For God is not unjust. He will not forget how hard you have worked for him and how you have shown your love to him by caring for other believers, as you still do.

HEBREWS 6:10 NLT

Burdens come in all varieties. You may think of specific trials, sins, misfortunes, or depression when you consider that word. Anything that weighs heavy or bogs down our brothers and sisters is a burden. So we are not off the hook when it comes to picking and choosing which difficulties we will assist them with. The author of these verses doesn't give us a list of which burdens to help carry. There are no degrees; He simply asks us to help shoulder the load.

Here is our chance to practice supportive charity. No other act can encourage like the sharing of burdens. Even the smallest gesture is a welcomed relief to those who feel alone in their struggle or pain. This truly fulfills the law of Christ to love one another as we do ourselves.

You can relate to oppression from your own experience. No one has escaped it completely. The most wonderful effect of reaching out in this way is that it touches you, too. You have been blessed to see the gratitude on the face of someone who was lifted by your gesture, and it feeds your own soul to know you are following Christ's example. What a privilege to be an extension of His grace and mercy, yet also receiving the same for ourselves when we desperately need it.

This request to stoop and reach out is an ongoing practice. Oppression will be with God's children always. We stick with the call to assist no matter how long it takes and for the rest of our lives.

Praise God for those who come alongside.

There remains then, for us all, the ascent toward higher things—which begins when we decide to love as far as it is possible to men to love.

DAVID HAZARD, *EARLY WILL I SEEK YOU*

Only This
Will Last

Only Because of Christ

Love never fails. But where there are prophecies, they will cease; where there are tongues, they will be stilled; where there is knowledge, it will pass away. For we know in part and we prophesy in part, but when completeness comes, what is in part disappears.

1 CORINTHIANS 13:8–10 NIV

We live, we love, we grow and learn. Through all these things we find out how to love and why we must. The total understanding of our commission to love God and others seems complex at times, yet we feel the tug in our hearts to belong to the very origin of all that we are to do for one another. It comes not from a feeling or a habit of benevolence. Love lives and breathes in us only because of our relationship with Christ.

How else could we be able to set aside self, anger, strife, and malice? It is the living God in us who expresses charity, enabling us to act out this thing called love. Our ability to birth a true representation of God's character is due to the seed of charity planted in us as we joined with Jesus as God's heirs.

The manifestation of this relationship with the Son of God is what we must nurture and feed. We can only be true to the commission to love when we are actively seeking His righteousness. We would not have access to it without Christ's sacrifice and His invitation to partake in the death of self and be adorned with the garland of grace.

Loving, serving, sacrifice, honor, and kindness can all be done without Christianity. But only what passes through the hands of charity will last. Only what is birthed out of our relationship with God, who *is* love, will affect eternity.

Simple Truth

———— ✦ ————

Therefore, we never stop thanking God that when you received his message from us, you didn't think of our words as mere human ideas. You accepted what we said as the very word of God—which, of course, it is. And this word continues to work in you who believe.

1 THESSALONIANS 2:13 NLT

We have tried to explain God, figure Him out, and then explain Him again. Never satisfied with the simplicity of God's Word, philosophical and ideological people want to find the hidden meaning to life, God, and salvation. Some might go so far as to reinvent Him or attribute to Him things that are not His design. We long for simple reasoning about how God is working in our lives.

Jesus came to us to tell us the simple truth about the Father. He spoke in parables that simple people could understand. Yet, even with the perfect completion of God standing in their midst, some felt the need to dissect His motives and twist His words. If they could misinterpret His message while in His presence, how much more are we doing so today?

Elaborate exposition of Jesus' deity and God's Word can get us into trouble. Fortunately, all that will disappear when the Complete One returns. Everything will be clear, and we won't depend on our own philosophy anymore. Anything man can conjure up concerning God's mysteries is only a feather of understanding—it will be carried off by the first breeze of glory when the heavens open up.

Find a quiet place to listen to the voice of the Holy Spirit within you. Then test it with God's Word. He will show you the truth in simple communion with Him. The rest—the words of man, the imaginings of philosophers—will all pass away in the end. Now is the time to trust in the simple truths God has specifically for you. He is preparing you for bigger things to come.

Take It with You

May you experience the love of Christ,
though it is too great to understand fully.
Then you will be made complete with all the
fullness of life and power that comes from God.

EPHESIANS 3:19 NLT

Love is a basic attribute of God. God is eternal, so therefore is love. Love will usher us into eternity. We will travel light, as love is all we will need. It's the only thing we have that will fit into heaven's theme. God will be the center attraction, and we will see immediately how awesome His love is for us.

We cannot comprehend what it means to be in the actual presence of perfect love. We have never and will never experience it fully until all the unrighteousness and sin is stripped from us. Those things will be no more when Jesus returns. How blessed we are to be released from those chains to participate in perfection. We will see that all the other things we cling to will be heavy, unnecessary baggage, and that even the biggest love we have will never withstand the test of heaven.

You may have had times in your life when you thought love was used as a whip against you, or that love was only a tool to manipulate you. There is great pain associated with the word, and the thought of an unfailing love is inconceivable to you. You are not alone. Many have experienced ugly and cruel things in the name of love. But you can trust God's love because it is who He is. It's not like the world's love.

When we are finally rid of the misconceptions, negative attitudes, and distortions of love, our eyes will behold all that is good and wonderful about it. No more mysteries, only pure love.

Want to See More?

—◆—

I will lead the blind by ways they have not
known, along unfamiliar paths I will guide them;
I will turn the darkness into light before them
and make the rough places smooth. These are
the things I will do; I will not forsake them.

Isaiah 42:16 NIV

The human mind is incredibly complex. We can create, imagine, and learn all at the same time because our intricate brains are so fearfully and wonderfully made. Our visual acuity is a wonder in its own right, run by a specific portion of the brain. In familiar surroundings, we can maneuver in the dark, feeling our way by internal visuals left over from seeing in the light of day. We don't have to see with perfect clarity in order to get from point A to point B.

Partial vision or partial knowledge of our circumstances is sometimes all we need to trust God. Faith takes over when sight fails, and we are accustomed to living out our Christian walk this way. Women have the added benefit of intuition, a special gift from our Creator.

Still, as children of God, we long to know more. It's the end of the story that invites us to stay with the book. We know God is faithful and our confidence is increased daily, keeping us stable in a crazy world. Through the days when we feel we are standing on a slippery slope, we hold out our hands for Him to take hold and pull us to sanity. He steadies us in the blackness of life when we lose patience with its progression.

His promises to lead you through to the perfect end will sustain you. He will reveal all things in His time as you ready yourself to receive them. Until then you must wait and trust Him with the light of day and your darkest nights.

I'll Be with You Soon

When Christ, who is your life, appears,
then you also will appear with him in glory.
COLOSSIANS 3:4 NIV

Letters from the front lines straggled in over the years,
signed always with the same sentiment—*I'll be with
you soon.* She joined wives all over the world who
waited for their loved ones to be back in their arms
again. Separation only proved to her that she was
incomplete without her mate. Somehow, across the
ocean, his heart called to her. Life didn't make sense
until he came home to be with her again.

We live life waiting to experience fullness, but it
never seems to come. God is withholding the full light
of knowledge, treasuring the moment when He can
show us all the mysteries of life and death. When He
returns to us, we will be complete, and life's trials and
challenges will finally make sense. We will see how
much we have gained and the future will be revealed.

Just as the wife waits with hope and anticipation, saving her love to pour on him when he comes home, we eagerly await His coming and prepare ourselves and those around us by proclaiming His promises. Our eyes will be opened then to the answers about love, sacrifice, and service. We will see the comparison of eternal outcomes and the efforts that were wasted because they did not stem from love.

You may be longing for fullness of understanding. You wish you could turn on a switch and illuminate the issues that cause pain and sorrow. But you must wait. We all must wait with joyous anticipation for Jesus to return and the light of knowledge to make full that which is half empty.

Keep hoping and expecting. He will be with you soon.

Sit at His Feet

---

*Oh, how great are God's riches and wisdom
and knowledge! How impossible it is for
us to understand his decisions and his ways!*

ROMANS 11:33 NLT

It's hard to comprehend that what we know of this life
is so incomplete, that when Christ returns and all is
revealed, the knowledge we depended on will disappear into insignificance. We have such confidence in
what we have learned about Him and His Word, we
may not consider that there is so much more we need
to know. Is this comforting or frightening? Maybe
some of both.

Our imaginations cannot dream what it will be
like when all that's familiar will pass away and new life,
new thoughts, and new understanding will be ours. All
our insecurities and confusion will cease to exist, for the
new knowledge will answer any and all questions and
mysteries. When the time is right and God chooses to
complete His plan, perfection will finally rule.

If you are a person who seeks knowledge, this may satisfy a longing. The reality of a revelation of this magnitude might excite you. It should. The more you learned, the more questions presented themselves, and now they will all be answered.

To sit at the feet of Jesus and hear the explanations to the issues that have plagued your soul will be a great joy. You will bask in the light that shines on every darkness, for all eternity. How wonderful to know you will never want for knowledge again.

We serve the living God who wants to share all He is. Be expecting. The time of the great reveal will come just as He promised.

Then You Will Know

For the earth will be filled with the knowledge of the glory of the LORD as the waters cover the sea.

HABAKKUK 2:14 NIV

When you think of heaven, what do you see in your mind? Most would likely list all their favorite activities or valued gifts they hope will be in abundance. Others might remember a time when they were at a peak spiritually and hope to be in that perpetual state. Or some might not dare to imagine what it will be like when they finally reach their eternal home.

Everything we fix our hope on here and now will be swallowed up in a new light and new knowledge. As everything about God and His attributes is shown to us, nothing will be left for imagination or wondering. There will be an eternal future, and we will have no worries about what is to come. All that is temporal. It will be time for eternal awareness.

You are living a life of uncertainty, even when you are confident of spiritual things. This is because you can only see a glimpse of what will be, a shadow of the entire truth. You can rest in that uncertainty. It is part of the wonder of life with God. He will be your rock, but He won't be fully known to you until you meet Him face-to-face. Then you will know all there is to know.

How humbling it is to think that Almighty God invites us to come and witness the reveal. You will have a front-row seat. Still uncertain? Yes, but your uncertainty is laced with anticipation, like a bride waiting for her bridegroom.

He will come and then you will know.

Shining Truth

—◆—

Dear friends, we are already God's children,
but he has not yet shown us what we will be like
when Christ appears. But we do know that we
will be like him, for we will see him as he really is.

1 JOHN 3:2 NLT

Remember back to when you fell in love, how much you wanted to be as close as possible to that person. You wanted to know everything there was to know about him and understand his thoughts. It's as if you wished to be one person, thinking and acting the same. This is what you thought would make you complete, union with someone you loved.

No matter how much effort we put into our relationships, we can never really slip inside another's skin and absorb their DNA. We can't be immersed in their thoughts or be their likeness. This is our limitation as humans.

We may think we are knit closely with Jesus, knowing His thoughts and hearing His voice. But how much more will we share in His likeness when He returns to show us all things on earth and in heaven, and more importantly, about Himself as our God, brother, and counselor.

Since you are not yet complete, hold on, wait for the day when you can take one look at His face and see clearly all the things you thought were clear before. Everything will shine with truth, having been shown to you directly from God.

He promised long ago that He would come back to turn on the lights and show us His glory. To be in His presence will be worth all trials and present humiliations. As the apostles were amazed to finally recognize the risen Jesus, we will be in awe when we are presented to the returning King.

We look forward to seeing Him in all His holiness, a relationship to last for all eternity.

Every Good Gift

For this reason I remind you to fan into flame the gift of God, which is in you through the laying on of my hands.

2 TIMOTHY 1:6 NIV

God has given us tools to live this Christian life until He returns. Without these tools and the Holy Spirit's comfort and guidance, we would struggle to edify and be edified. Gifts of prophecy and knowledge help us maintain our faith in the community of believers. We need all the gifts of the Spirit to be in use because we do not yet have perfection in faith. We don't even know what that looks like.

Assembling the family calendar, planning menus, deciphering what the children need on a daily basis are all gifts a woman draws upon to run a happy home. But when the children are gone and we are left completely alone, those kinds of gifts are no longer needed. Life has changed and the only person we have to manage is ourselves. Since there is no guesswork at taking care of our own needs, once-valuable gifts used to organize the family unit are obsolete.

This reality is so unfamiliar, it's a stretch of faith to believe He will replace all our gifts with full understanding. Pride, talents, and competition will pass away. There will be no need for special gifts because the perfect gift will encompass eternity. In this perfect world, no assistance will be needed, growth will be complete, and there will be no uncertain future to predict.

We won't miss specific gifts as we bask in the glory of perfection. Use your gifts wisely while you have them, and rejoice that someday they will be useless!

Eternal Identity

So we fix our eyes not on what is seen,
but on what is unseen, since what is seen
is temporary, but what is unseen is eternal.

2 CORINTHIANS 4:18 NIV

We are learning that most things are temporal. In light of the awesomeness of God and the glory to be revealed in heaven, what can stand the test of time? We seldom ask ourselves this question. Living each day as it comes is the pattern that is generated by busy schedules and unknown futures. We either look too close or too far away and never know which time and space to live in. Both are attractive in their own way, but neither is very satisfying on its own.

We depend on the things that we know and assume they will always be there. Money, family, skills, and gifts, we consider them all a part of us. But these things are temporary. We will eventually be without them as they exist now. Still we incorporate them so tightly into our identity, it's hard to imagine a time when they will be gone.

We cannot attribute eternal significance to temporal things and still draw near to the only thing that will last for all time. God is spirit, God is light, God is and was and always will be. And God is love. We find our eternal identity only in Him. When we can associate our eternal soul with Him, we will filter all that we do through eternal thinking, and earthly things won't carry the weight they once did.

If we sustain our identity in the fleeting things of this world, we will be a stranger in a strange land. Heaven doesn't need the transient possessions we want to take, and we won't need them either.

Loosen your grip on them and look up.

Growth is the goal of the Christian.
Maturity is mandatory. If a child ceased
to develop, the parent would be concerned. . . .
When a child stops growing, something is wrong.

MAX LUCADO

Mature
Understanding

Baby Talk

When I was a child, I talked like a child, I thought like a child, I reasoned like a child. When I became a man, I put the ways of childhood behind me.

1 CORINTHIANS 13:11 NIV

A mother wraps her baby and holds him tight against her. She sings a lullaby, speaks tender words of love and dreams. The newborn is comforted by the sound of his mother's voice. When the child is old enough to react and respond, suddenly mother's language changes to baby talk, words and phrases that make no sense to anyone, except the mother. Then as the child matures, the baby talk gives way to grown-up language.

Who knows why we resort to this shift in communication. There is a time and place for baby talk. But eventually the baby must be taught the language of maturity. It's the only way he will get along in the world. Imagine trying to fit in when all you can speak is sweet silly gibberish. How would we ever be taken seriously?

God speaks to us, not in baby talk, but in pure words. His voice resonates in our minds and hearts and we recognize Him as our loving Father. If we want to do His will, we must hear His instructions clearly. As we grow spiritually, His voice becomes ingrained in our lives and our character. We expand our spiritual vocabulary to become more like Him, and as others see Him through us, the more effective we will be in a world lacking in mature leadership. Those new in the faith will look to us to teach them how to advance in their Christian lives. We have an opportunity to play a part in their personal growth, just as we participate in the lives of our children, encouraging them to crawl, walk, and then run.

Baby talk is fine for a time. But then it's time to grow in the language of the Father.

Retain the Wonder

———— ⋅•⋅ ————

He has caused his wonders to be remembered;
the LORD is gracious and compassionate.

PSALM 111:4 NIV

What happened to the wonder of our childhood? Our search for the explanation of life can leave us disillusioned and confused. We want someone to tell us why things work the way they do, and to make sense of a world that has no rhyme or reason. We walk through the land mines of life hoping to find meaning, and in the process we come away wounded. Is there anyone who can restore the awe of our childhood?

Yes, there is still room for wonder in our lives. Jesus brings back meaning and mystery to an otherwise boring existence. Without Him we would see only darkness. He longs to ask us the questions that keep us searching for answers. He could reveal everything to us if He willed, but the hunt for understanding is how we stay interested in our mission.

The child in us sees life at face value and accepts it. When we lose our childlike innocence we aren't able to process trials and disappointments with hope for a good outcome. A child trusts his parent to make everything turn out right. We must learn to trust our heavenly Father to mend our land-mine wounds and prove to us that life can still hold joy and mystery.

Life as a child is uncluttered and free, but it's not meant to last forever. We move on to bigger ways of loving, caring, ministering, and sharing our wonder with others. Jesus continues to reveal ways for us to retain our awe and worship as we press on.

His explanation of life is all we need.

Don't Look Back

—◆—

"How can someone be born when they are old?"
Nicodemus asked. "Surely they cannot enter
a second time into their mother's womb to be born!"

JOHN 3:4 NIV

Once we have a special relationship with Jesus, we will never want to return to our old lives. Or would we? Yes, our old life will always call to us because it is centered on us and not on God. It doesn't seem to matter what age we are, retreating into infancy feels good. Just when we think we have moved past the immaturity we tried so hard to outgrow, we slip into those childish ways.

There are risks to following Christ. If we were to count the cost through our own eyes, we might never make the choice to be born again. When we see through the filter of eternity and know the high calling we will reach, we will make the right choice. The cost of self-denial, service, and dedication to His commission will seem small compared to the alternative.

You were not born again just for you. Your new life is designed to bring all glory to God. Your old ways won't work for you anymore, and your old life is never going to satisfy again. Once we understand what it is to be a new creature, we begin to function with new ways to love and serve God and others.

The more we practice this new way, the closer we move toward God and away from our old self. Daily we choose our new life, daily we take the steps toward something bigger than ourselves and more wonderful than anything our previous life could have afforded.

Thanks be to God for all we have to look forward to.

A New Way of Thinking

—◆—

*Instead, let the Spirit renew your thoughts
and attitudes. Put on your new nature,
created to be like God—truly righteous and holy.*
EPHESIANS 4:23–24 NLT

You've heard it's a woman's prerogative to change her
mind. This is an expected behavior for our sex. It can
be a bad thing, frustrating to the people around you.
Or it can be a positive thing in the perspective of
spiritual maturity. You must at some point change your
mind about keeping your childish thinking or choosing to grow up. The choice is yours to make: childish
attitudes or productive adult words and deeds.

Accepting Christ is only the first step. In order to reach the heights of perfection God hopes for us, we must put on a new way of thinking. We surrender our past, trust Him with our future, and give Him the glory for our accomplishments. This is the sign to the world that His nature in us is what makes life worth living. We are to be true examples of His character, but we cannot be if we still have childlike thinking.

You will be tempted to change your mind again. Satan will attempt to twist your new attitudes with lies and coercion. But we cling to our new knowledge and new disposition as mature followers of Christ, not giving credence to things we now believe are false. Soon it is natural to see life with all its conflicts as God sees them.

What a relief it is not to be dependent on our self-made conclusions about life. With God's way of thinking we are secure in our minds, not needing to waver. The distraction of insecurity in our choices vanishes when we exchange it for the solid foundation of a renewed mind.

Come Let Us Reason

So if you're serious about living this new resurrection life with Christ, act like it. Pursue the things over which Christ presides. Don't shuffle along, eyes to the ground, absorbed with the things right in front of you. Look up, and be alert to what is going on around Christ—that's where the action is. See things from his perspective.

COLOSSIANS 3:1–2 MSG

We really do want to live right, be acceptable in God's sight, and walk continuously in God's Word. No one who knows Christ would choose to displease Him. Our heart's desire as mature Christians is to continually become more like Him. This is not possible if our minds are not renewed and infused with His good and perfect will.

It's hard work to throw off our old ways and put on the new. Our life's struggle to know Him better, learn His will, and grow in grace and integrity is not the easy way. It's long and narrow and has many twists and turns. We can only stay on course when we concentrate on spiritual matters. There is a war going on between our sense of reality and the active, living Word of God. Therefore, the more we focus on God's instruction, the less likely we are to fall for the falsehood of our own reasoning.

As women we are drawn to reason, but to live daily for Him, we must see and reason the way He does. Prayer, meditation, and stillness are required in order to shut out the world and all its distortion. Our reasoning doesn't work for God, and it cannot accomplish His will for us.

The days disappear and our lives seem like a vapor. Draw closer to God than you ever have before. Now is the time for renewed reasoning. It will sustain you in hard times and give you understanding you never thought possible.

Journey of Change

———— ✦ ————

*I am certain that God, who began the good work
within you, will continue his work until it is finally
finished on the day when Christ Jesus returns.*

PHILIPPIANS 1:6 NLT

We abandon the most important journey of our lives
if we abandon change. To be "born again" means we
are starting a new life, and we must follow the road
to growth and productivity that He has placed before
us. As a babe must learn to change from milk to solid
food, so must we change our diets in order to mature.
This is only the first of many changes to be made in
our walk with Christ.

How easily we give up. Something shiny attracts
our attention and soon we find we have detoured from
our journey or stopped moving completely. If we aren't
moving forward, we aren't really gaining any ground at
all. We must never be satisfied with standing still.

There is great danger in this attitude. When we cease to see the need for growth, we will abandon the journey and may never resume it.

Think of how sad you would be to see your child's growth stunted, his stature forever stuck. You would give anything to see him enjoy full maturity in body and do all the activities you had planned for him. Sure, he will learn to make do, and it will seem normal after a while. But still, you will wonder what could have been.

Our Creator will always choose for us to be full grown and able to do anything He has planned. Don't abandon the journey. It's never the right choice to give up before you have reached your destiny. Keep your eyes on Him and He will gently nudge you in the right direction.

Peter Pan Living

God wants us to grow up, to know the whole truth and tell it in love—like Christ in everything. We take our lead from Christ, who is the source of everything we do.
EPHESIANS 4:15 MSG

On December 27, 1904, a play written by novelist J. M. Barrie was presented on the stage for the first time in Westminster, England. The play was titled *The Boy Who Wouldn't Grow Up*, but we all know it as *Peter Pan*, the story about a boy who wanted to remain a child to avoid the trials and responsibilities of adulthood. Children all over the world can relate to his passion for play and freedom. Most adults can relate, too.

When growing up seems too tough or demanding, we would like to sail away to Never Land and leave our cares behind. As mature Christians we set aside that option when we choose to accept what God has for us. Staying childlike in our spiritual walk hurts us and those we are responsible for. The temporary joys of childhood freedom must come to an end.

When our spiritual growth stagnates, we are no longer a solution to the problems in our families, our communities, or our world. We become part of the plague of self-seeking attitudes that hinder the progress of God's message. Our need for attention and having our own way creates a kind of Christianity unremarkable and undesirable in the eyes of those we are to love and reach.

A Me World

No one should seek their own good,
but the good of others.

1 CORINTHIANS 10:24 NIV

"Mine, mine." That is the motto of the nursery clan. Mothers cringe when they see their sweet little child grab a toy from another child, declaring ownership and staking his claim. The child's world extends only as far as he can reach. This is our birthright, selfishness. It takes years of quality parenting to wean the little ones off the bottle of self and train them in the fine art of sharing.

This is the Father's job. He gently guides us away from our self-centered nature and shows us a new way to live. Day by day He waits patiently for us to give up our ground and let someone else have a turn at first dibs. He is as proud as any parent when we show signs of compassion and caring. He gives a nod of approval when we share our bounty with those who are less fortunate.

These things are the indication that we have left behind the childish inclinations that stunt our growth and cause the lost to turn up their noses at Christianity. When we can share without giving it a second thought, not only does the world notice, but we will know we are closer to reflecting His character—we have reached yet another level of maturity.

Your success at forsaking the "mine, mine" syndrome is only because of the work of Christ in your life. You have Him to thank for guiding you beyond the Me world. Now it is your turn to share the good news—you don't have to live in childlike selfishness anymore.

It Happens to Everyone

---

*I know what I'm doing. I have it all planned out—
plans to take care of you, not abandon you,
plans to give you the future you hope for.*

JEREMIAH 29:11 MSG

We all have to grow up sometime. We cannot stop our
bodies from maturing, changing shape, or showing
age. They will fail us and leave us with no choice but
to move on to our eternal home. Our souls and our
personal legacy will live on.

You may have asked yourself what your children and
your children's children will believe about you after you
are gone. You hope they will remember you cared more
about excellence than power, that you gave more than
you took, that you knew how to love, and that God was
in control of your life. This is not accomplished if we
refuse to walk the path He has chosen for us.

As adults, we should be accustomed to trusting. This is one childlike characteristic we need to carry throughout our lives. Knowing for certain God has a plan for us prepares us to live the kind of lives we would be proud to have modeled. What a comfort to know that our Father will never leave us. What a joy to taste of the hope He has for us. This is the legacy we leave to the ones we are responsible to raise up. The fruit a good life bears will leave seeds of trust in God, who holds the blueprint for the generation that comes after us.

It's not the passing of time that determines our maturity, it's the proof of God's existence found in a lifetime of obedience. We follow His plan to the very end and reap life everlasting.

We must mirror God's love in the midst of a world full of hatred. We are the mirrors of God's love, so we may show Jesus by our lives.

CORRIE TEN BOOM

A Clear Reflection

Face-to-Face

For now we see only a reflection as in a mirror;
then we shall see face to face. Now I know in part;
then I shall know fully, even as I am fully known.

1 CORINTHIANS 13:12 NIV

"You can't come in until you are cleaned up." How
often have we said this to our children, especially boys?
Their escapades outside can leave them dusty and
muddy. If we let them in they will leave a mess in the
house. For us, that is unacceptable. But once the dirt
is shaken from their clothes and the mud washed off
their boots, they may come in.

So it is with our heavenly Father. We may long to see Him face-to-face, but we are not ready as long as we are in a sinful state. When the end of this life comes, we will enter heaven clean and upright. Only then will we be acceptable to meet our holy and perfect God. He cannot embrace us until we have crossed from sinful man to spotless child.

As King and Creator, it's the only way He can receive you. If you were invited to attend a state dinner for the king of another country, you would have to follow the protocol necessary to meet him. You wouldn't want to show up without proper dress or etiquette. You would of course make every attempt to meet his approval.

Right now it doesn't seem conceivable that we could be good enough, but the veil of sin will be stripped away someday. It's not enough to put our best foot forward, behave nicely, or say all the right things in His presence. It is because of His mercy and grace that we will be allowed to stand to face Him.

Prepare to See

However, as it is written: "What no eye has seen,
what no ear has heard, and what no human
mind has conceived"—the things God has
prepared for those who love him.

1 CORINTHIANS 2:9 NIV

Looking at someone's photograph isn't nearly as good as seeing them in person. Their features are affected by sunlight, distance, and camera quality. It's frustrating to tell someone about how pretty your daughter is and then not be able to find a photo that is a true representation of her beauty.

We catch glimpses of God through His creation, His people, and His miracles. But it's as if we see them in a distorted reflection. We have to filter all those impressions through our humanity and limited vision. Hard as we may try, we will never be able to see clearly until we are in the heavenly place that He prepares for us.

In turn, we must prepare to go. We must do it with limited sight and unperfected faith. We lean on the gift of His grace to help us in this time on earth, knowing it will carry us into His throne room. Our perception of His love will be transformed into a reality we cannot yet fully see.

You can prepare for this new reality by seeking God and asking Him to reveal the secrets of His character. He will show you glimpses to draw you near to Himself, a place of shelter and learning. A place where you can anticipate the joys of your eternal home.

He waits to present you with a clear vision of His wonders. He is ready to show you. Prepare to go, prepare to see.

Look to Me

---

*And he who searches our hearts knows the mind
of the Spirit, because the Spirit intercedes for God's
people in accordance with the will of God.*

ROMANS 8:27 NIV

Our life's story isn't always a pretty one. There are
days when we wonder how certain situations will be
resolved and how much good can come out of misery
and pain. We toil in work, relationships, health, and
wealth. Loose ends abound and it seems that some
things will never come to a satisfactory resolution. We
ask God if He knows or cares about our problems. He
answers, "I know. Keep looking to Me."

You may be wondering if God is fully acquainted with the issues that plague you. While you are trying so desperately to understand why things happen the way they do, His silence seems to suggest He is unaware of how you feel and who you are. But you know better. He knows you fully and someday you will see and know Him fully, too.

We want to see everything clearly right now, but we must hold on awhile longer. When He decides the time is right for us to know all, He will shine light in the dark places. Then we will see Him for who He is, a sovereign God who has known about all of us, our struggles, our triumphs, and our pain. When we see Him in that light, our vision will be crystal clear. All our questions will be answered in a moment.

Trust Him at His word that He knew you before you were born. When it feels like He is not to be found, when it seems He is far away, imagine the day when you will look at Him in His holiness. He will no longer be just a reflection.

Imagine the day when your soul will finally be at rest.

Full-Grown Knowledge

---

*"I knew you before I formed you in your mother's
womb. Before you were born I set you apart
and anointed you as my prophet to the nations."*

JEREMIAH 1:5 NLT

The love and hope we have for our children is as a
grain of sand compared to the love and hope God
has for His children. Before we become parents, our
understanding of God's sacrifice and care for us is in
the shadows of our minds. We know with our heads
that He has shown mercy and grace by saving us for
heaven. But becoming a parent sinks that knowledge
from our head to our hearts.

Anyone who is responsible for another human being, whether through blood or adoption or guardian-
ship, longs to be loved by the one in their care. So the
Father longs for our devotion and trust. He knows us
as no one else can know us.

The relationship between you and God may be colored by your relationship with your earthly father. You may have been treated like a princess, or abused, or experienced lots of broken promises. If you grew up without a dad, you may have felt abandoned by him. You could be missing so much if you have not given God the benefit of the doubt. He has so much He wants to give you.

God knew and loved you long before you were in your mother's womb. He formed you for relationship with Him. The child is gone, but the grown-up that remains is capable of a new understanding, a heart understanding. You can be sure He has loved you out of His intimate knowledge of you. His plans for you are exceedingly grander than any of your dreams.

Embrace Him as His grown-up child, and some-day you will know Him in all fullness.

He Has Chosen You

---

*For we are God's masterpiece. He has created
us anew in Christ Jesus, so we can do the
good things he planned for us long ago.*
EPHESIANS 2:10 NLT

Just as surely as God loves you, He knows the deepest
region of your heart. The relationship is incomplete
as long as we are here on earth, but His love for us is
complete. The world doesn't understand the love of
God. We must tell them, paint a picture of Him by
the way we interact with others. We live out His love
for us, hoping to be an honorable representation and
reflection. As we effectively reflect the awesome God
we serve, the world will embrace Him, desiring to
know Him fully.

The image many have about God is that He hovers over the earth waiting to pounce on sinners and dole out punishment. This reveals how little we really know Him. As His ambassadors we demonstrate patience, grace, and love. We want very much for others to experience the love of God and the blessings of Jesus in their lives just as we have. We must find a way to tell them God knows them intimately and wants a relationship with them.

What has Jesus done for you? Share it. How big is your God? Tell it. You are His workmanship and were created in His image. It is your privilege to reveal His qualities by the way you reach out and by the depth of your experience with His loving care. Are they watching, are they listening? Yes. And we will be true to our calling and responsibility to represent the God who will save them.

He knows you and He has chosen you. Soon you will understand all His mysteries.

Not So Distant

---•◆•---

*But as for me, how good it is to be near God! I have
made the Sovereign LORD my shelter, and I will
tell everyone about the wonderful things you do.*

PSALM 73:28 NLT

If you have known God for some time, you may have
settled into a certain way of thinking about Him. He
seems like a distant figure, off running the universe
with a wave of His hand. You may have associated His
persona with that of your earthly father, or believed
Him to be like the pictures in the Bible you had as a
child. Some days it seems silly to try and reach God
when He is so far away or unapproachable.

We look at the clouds in the sky and wonder if He is there somewhere looking down on us. Can we ever reach Him, and can He ever be real to us? Our vision is dimmed, filtered by life and lack of knowledge. We are satisfied to let Father God stay just beyond our reach. After all, His Son, Jesus, is the One whom we are to know personally.

Jesus came to reveal to us the Father—His Father. It's not possible to know one without knowing the other, but we must never be content to believe God is out of our reach. He patiently waits for His children to come to Him. He is never so distant that He can't be real to us, and never so busy that He can't spend time with us.

God has ordained a Father-child relationship between Himself and you. His motivation for wanting you to know Him comes from His unquenchable love for you. Distance is not His idea of fellowship.

He doesn't live in the clouds. He is close enough for you to see Him if you open your eyes.

Welcome Home

So God created mankind in his own image, in the image of God he created them; male and female he created them.

GENESIS 1:27 NIV

Since God's face is still hidden from the world, He is often judged not by His word or deeds, but by our personal experiences, good or bad. Our finite minds cannot comprehend the ways of God, and we are inclined to lean on our limited view of Him.

The truth is that the image of God walks the earth in you and every other person. Whether we are good or bad or very bad, we still bear the mark of God on our lives. He created us in His image and there is nothing we can do about it. Just as our children resemble us, we also have that family resemblance of our heavenly Father.

Are we pious enough to believe that the most heinous criminal does not also bear God's DNA? How fortunate for us that He rejects no one because of their personality or deeds. They are still offered the same gifts we are offered. This is the hope we have until we are in His presence. No matter where we are or what we have done, He will melt away our shame and all the confusing messages about Him will be put to rest. We will see on His countenance how much He loves us and how much He loves the rest of humanity.

No one will be good or bad. We'll all stand on an equal plane of sinfulness. Restoration and reconciliation will cause us all to fall at His feet in gratitude. Each redeemed child will be welcomed to a familiar home.

While We Wait

—— ⚬※⚬ ——

But the exact day and hour? No one knows that, not
even heaven's angels, not even the Son. Only the Father.
So keep a sharp lookout, for you don't know the timetable.
MARK 13:32 MSG

Many generations of Christian people have believed
theirs was the last before the Lord returned. It seemed
that time was running out and heaven was just
around the corner. But we are all still here, and there
is much left to do and to learn. Although our home
is heaven and experiencing fullness of the Father our
goal, we have a purpose to fulfill while we wait for
that time.

You may have unrealized dreams. Now is the time to move toward them, to nurture them into being. God planted them in your heart, and while there is breath in you, there is still a gift of time for you to enjoy. Not only will you have more chances to discover your unique purpose, there is opportunity to worship, serve, and perfect your faith.

Many of us have lists of things we wanted to do or accomplish in our lives. Some have never checked off a single item, while others are adding more. Our pursuits are not always God ordained. We waste time and spiritual energy on our own rabbit trails of satisfaction. If we respect the time we've been gifted with, our eyes will be open to see the work to be done. Only the Father knows when our toil will come to an end; we see only part of the picture now.

While we wait, we must keep an ear to God's voice and our eyes searching out dreams, answering our calling, and sharing knowledge of Him with the world. We don't know the time, we only know the fruit of our faith in Christ means eternally abiding with Him and the Father.

It will be worth the wait.

He Won't Disappoint

"Be still, and know that I am God!
I will be honored by every nation.
I will be honored throughout the world."

PSALM 46:10 NLT

The world is filled with people who are disappointed in God. Because they haven't investigated Him thoroughly, they build up in their minds what they think He ought to be and do. They are grieved at His lack of acceptable performance. They see only a stingy God who is distant and hard to please. It's too easy to buy into the notion that He is up there somewhere, not caring, too busy to notice our pain and suffering. But nothing could be further from the truth. This image is of our own making, the partial vision we have come to accept.

We are here on this planet only by God's grace, and we enjoy free will. We are free to know our Father or reject Him. The courtship is over, and He waits for us to accept His proposal to live eternally with Him. How fortunate we are to be given chance after chance to delve into the character of God who deserves our worship.

Foolish is the man or woman who settles for the picture of God that is anything but magnificent, benevolent, awesome, and personal. We can't set Him any lower than the highest level of light and love. Our finite minds can only imagine His height and breadth and width. But the limits of our imaginations will be removed someday. Then there will be confirmation that our loyalties were not unfounded and that He is indeed so much more than we imagined.

We will see just how big our perception of God has been. Our bewilderment of His ways will be explained in His countenance. Don't you long to hear Him beckon you to come in and discover the truth of your existence?

Power in Knowledge

—— ✦ ——

The heart of the discerning acquires knowledge,
for the ears of the wise seek it out.
PROVERBS 18:15 NIV

There are days when you feel you have nothing to offer
anyone. Strength is drained by the demands of life and
the onslaught of negativity from a disheartened world.
You may ask, "What's the use? It's all coming to an end
someday and who will care?" You strive to know more
and to understand situations that have you baffled.
There seems to be no positive influence on your life, so
how are you to help someone who has desperate needs?

What are we to do when we don't have all the
answers? How do we press through the dim light to
achieve wisdom and usefulness?

Although full clarity is yet to come from God, we can still fulfill our mission to share the love and purposes of God. Giving up is not an option. We need the power of knowledge to fuel our hearts and minds. We have access to the voice of the Spirit to tell us the secret things that feed the souls of men and women everywhere. We depend on this knowledge to change failure into success, defeat into victory, and judgment into mercy.

Right now you are puzzled. You see the fog of sin and humanity and take a step back. No one wants to enter into the unknown without a weapon. Your weapon is knowledge of God and His ways, your message is the love of God. He did not leave you here alone to figure everything out for yourself, to do battle in a world that is against you. You can acquire confidence and boldness when armed with the knowledge of God in Christ Jesus.

*Do not let your happiness depend on
something you may lose. If love is to be
a blessing, not a misery, it must be for
the only Beloved who will never pass away.*

C. S. LEWIS

Embrace Eternity

Unending Supply

And now these three remain: faith, hope and love.
But the greatest of these is love.

1 CORINTHIANS 13:13 NIV

We live in a disposable world. Unlike our ancestors who had to use everything until it was of no use at all, we can simply throw anything away when it has lost its luster, lost its attraction, or lost its place on a cluttered shelf of other useless things. Society gives little value to things that are easily discarded. We can always get another one or trade it in on something newer and shinier. Most items are not built to last these days—at least that's what we perceive.

So we lean not on the perishable things in life lest we fall. Only what God has ordained to last will be with us through eternity. Faith, hope, and love are all that's left when the world takes everything else from us.

In times of doubt we lean instead on His promises. His Word assures us that our future is not a mystery to Him and that He will provide the elements we need to survive heartache, confusion, or even physical distress. Our time here is very short, but we have the ability to accumulate all the riches of His promises. Faith is our foundation, hope is our encouragement, and love is God in us. What more could we need?

You can find meaning for every part of your life in these three elements. As you learn the value of each, you will see how clearly they represent His character, His plan, and His immortality. He freely gives them all to you. Faith may waver, hope gets deferred—but love is the all-encompassing reflection of God.

As for love, you have a vast supply of the greatest gift. It will take you forever to use it up!

Love Extravagantly

She did what she could. She poured perfume
on my body beforehand to prepare for my burial.
MARK 14:8 NIV

Not too many people who interacted with Jesus during
His time on earth showered Him with extravagant
love. Mostly it was the women who saw the Father in
Him, who responded to the agape love in His countenance and words. They responded in return with acts
of love and worship.

The woman in this scripture is perhaps the most
well-remembered. She shamelessly offered her love and
worship in such a way that it shocked and appalled the
people who were closest to Him. Even those who had
settled in their minds that Jesus was the Son of God
had only contempt for a woman who would give Jesus
His due praise. Had they truly known the value of this
act, they would have stood in line to bear Him homage.

Extravagant love requires death to any doubts and an elevation of humility. It takes risk. This is why it is rare. When we realize the cost, we are reluctant to give extravagantly. To pour out our most precious possession, love, means we must forgive, show mercy, and open ourselves up to be hurt. Yet Christ's example to us is enough to break our fears and inhibitions. We are free to lavish on Him and our brothers and sisters the life-giving love that will last forever.

Take care not to be stingy with love. If you feel you are lacking, remember it is by the power of Christ in you that you are able to show love. Of all the gifts you could give—love is the best.

The Bond of Hope

Therefore, we who have fled to him for refuge can have great confidence as we hold to the hope that lies before us. This hope is a strong and trustworthy anchor for our souls. It leads us through the curtain into God's inner sanctuary.

Hebrews 6:18–19 NLT

If God has ever spoken to you, you have heard hope in His voice. He cannot speak without the whisper of the glory that lies before us. If He says it is true, that there is a dwelling place with Him for eternity, then our hope is never unfounded. It is the kind of confidence that can't be explained. It reaches our souls and points the way into the presence of God.

It's in the times when we need refuge that God meets us, holding out His hand of hope. This hope keeps us certain of His intentions, convinced of His plan. To be offered hope of this magnitude is far beyond what we deserve. Yet, as with all His offerings, it is ours for the taking, ours to give to others.

We are bonded to Christ through the confidence we have of the glory to come. But more than that we have the power of courageous love to share hope to a world that longs for it, the needy and the dying, all who are a shadow of ourselves. They need what we have.

As our vision focuses on heaven and the hope of His glory, let us not neglect the blessing of spreading the good news. There is still time to peel back the layers of doubt and discouragement and expose the one thing that will anchor us to the truth. We shall behold Him, face-to-face. It's not a fairy tale, it's our reality. It's our hope.

Yes, Even Death

---

*For love is as strong as death, its jealousy
as enduring as the grave. Love flashes
like fire, the brightest kind of flame.*

SONG OF SOLOMON 8:6 NLT

There is an unquenchable fire in the center of God's
amazing love. It is not often captured in song or poem,
and sometimes it's tucked away as if it were heresy.
God's love is more than sweetness and song. The
fierceness of God's love is what has triumphed over
death and hell. If God's love had not endured death,
there would be no victory over the grave for us, and
no home in heaven. God Himself had to banish the
chains that would bind us for eternity.

You need this powerful love in your life more than you know. You battle every day for your faith, your children's faith, and the legacy of love you wish to leave. There is resistance to everything you do for God, and you need the power of love to win the little victories so vital to your peace and comfort, your joy in Christ.

As we dream of what is to come for all humankind, and for those who profess Christ as Lord, we cannot leave out love's fire. It plays an important role in determining who will survive the unforgiving force in the world. His fire warms us, and through it we are able to persevere in the midst of fear.

Nothing in heaven or earth can extinguish this fire of love. We can rest in the knowledge that when everything else has been consumed, God in all His glory, fire and flame, will still live within us. It will burn on in the legacy of love we leave to the next generations until time is no more.

Faith and Understanding

Jesus turned and saw her. "Take heart, daughter,"
he said, "your faith has healed you." And the
woman was healed at that moment.

MATTHEW 9:22 NIV

Faith accomplishes so many things. It takes on many titles: assurance, belief, conviction, or credibility. But when it is applied to our lives in a way that changes us, it becomes as tangible as a soft touch or a firm hug. There is much to worry about in this life; that's not likely to change. We will need faith in abundance as time closes in on the world. Those who have yet to believe will be watching for signs and miracles. Only the deepest faith will produce the proof they will require. Faith in action is the force of attraction we use to draw others to the saving knowledge of Christ. As we exercise faith in our lives, it will increase.

Augustine said this about faith: "Understanding is the reward of faith. Therefore seek not to understand that thou mayest believe, but believe that thou mayest understand."

When we listen to other voices concerning faith and following Christ, there is confusion and doubt. Our minds need understanding to make sense of our faith life, but believing is what opens the door for understanding. The Father waits for us to practice our faith by believing He will do what He says He will do.

With faith comes optimism. With optimism comes hope. These gifts from God hold us up while we try to manage our lives. He will provide the understanding and the increase. He has promised to sustain us by His love. As we set aside our worry and look to Him, we find out just how He values our faith.

Live the Love Moments

"I have loved you with an everlasting love;
I have drawn you with unfailing kindness."

JEREMIAH 31:3 NIV

What makes love so effective is that is doesn't spring from our own well of emotion. Love is rooted in the heart and character of God. If we expect human love to be the catalyst for service to others, we will fail. If we embrace the knowledge that love is from God and is eternal, perfect, and complete, we can love from His heart.

Since God's love is all these things, we know it could never disappear. Its origin and essence are not fragile. Love is the quality and structure of our faith. There is nothing that can stand against the love of God. Although we may be attacked on every side by evil, it cannot penetrate the fortress of love's power.

What does this mean for your daily life? It means if you are joined with the heart of God and are purposefully aware of love's influence, you can accomplish anything. You can glean strength and power by basking in the light of His love hour by hour. Love teaches, repairs, soothes, encourages, and guides. Love is what you need to make it through the days and weeks of your hectic life.

Far beyond our daily living is the eternal state of love. This love encompasses all time, space, and reason. It is the answer to all our questions and the reason we are able to someday stand in His presence.

Live in love's moment through your life in Jesus. It's the bond between you that will never break.